17/2/92   33825   JD (JEN)

WITHDRAWN

SMALL BUSINESSES

HOW TO SUCCEED & SURVIVE

⌐RIDGE

.dge
⌐erkhamsted
Hertfordshire HP4 1NS
United Kingdom

Telephone +44 (0)1442 841160
Facsimile +44 (0)1442 841211

⌐n below

011156E1

Parker
Inv- 5245525

OBSERVER · Touche Ross

SMALL BUSINESSES

HOW TO SUCCEED & SURVIVE

Brian Jenks

Foreword by Eric Forth MP
Preface by Melvyn Marckus

Headway · Hodder & Stoughton

Cover and text illustrations: Joe Cummings

British Library Cataloguing in Publication Data

Jenks, Brian
    Small businesses: How to succeed and survive.
    I. Title   II. The Observer   III. Touche Ross
    658.02

ISBN 0 340 55652 8

First published 1991

Typeset by Columns Design and Production Services Ltd, Reading
Printed in Great Britain for the education publishing division of Hodder &
Stoughton Ltd, Mill Road, Dunton Green, Sevenoaks, Kent by Biddles Ltd,
Guildford, Surrey

CONTENTS

Preface by Melvyn Marckus   vii

Foreword by Eric Forth MP   ix

Introduction   xi

Start-up
    Are you an entrepreneur?   3
    How Gordon failed   8
    How Jeremy succeeded   12

Partnership or company?
    Partnerships   19
    The limited way to enjoy your own
        company   24

Planning for success
    Think before you leap   31
    Blueprint for a business   34
    Cash flow is king   39
    Good housekeeping   42

Advice
    You and your accountant   47
    Professional advisers   50

Banks
    Learn to love your bank manager   57
    Bankers beware   60

Government help
    The network   67
    The Loan Guarantee Scheme   71
    Beauty of the BES   75
    Make the best of BES   78

Nothing ventured
    Venture capital   83
    Nothing ventured, nothing gained   87
    Going public   94

Management
    Team work and succession   103
    Casual employment   108
    Business insurance   113
    The high-tech jungle   118
    VAT: it pays to get it right   122
    Crisis management   126

Training
    Training for success   133

Alternative finance
    All the fun of the franchise   139
    Franchises: how to cut a fair deal   144
    Buying a business from the receiver   148
    Factoring   152

Marketing
    Marketing   159
    You and 1992   164

Tough times
    Why firms go bust   171
    Banks and the recession   176
    Making the best of a bad debt   181
    How to avoid bad debts   186
    Directors in danger   191

Self-preservation
    Employed or self-employed?   199
    Remuneration or dividend?   203
    Separate taxation   209
    Pensions for professionals   213
    The director's dilemma   216
    Action man in retirement   221

Small firms' organisations   225

PREFACE

I first met Brian Jenks, Touche Ross's doyen of small business, in the Autumn of 1984. *The Observer* was poised to launch its first business supplement, a two-part survey entitled *How to Start Your Own Business*, and I was eager to draw on Touche's expertise.

We agreed on a collaborative venture; a rather grand description of an arrangement whereby Brian wrote the majority of the articles which, as he sat alongside me at *The Observer*, I edited.

Accountants and journalists are not necessarily a natural mix but, as we produced the survey in the Spring of 1985, I was struck by the ease with which Brian adapted to the deadline-dominated environment of a newspaper. Few accountants would have coped; Brian thrived.

In the event, *How to Start Your Own Business* attracted a substantial response and proved the forerunner of a host of *Observer Business* supplements.

Last year, *Observer Business* introduced a weekly column – 'Unquoted' – targeted specifically at the proprietors of small businesses. Not surprisingly, I again asked Brian to take up his pen.

Brian's pen covered a multitude of subjects: articles which ranged from relationships with bank managers to the Business Expansion Scheme; from business plans to crisis management.

Once again *The Observer* received a significant response; Brian's advice was clearly in demand. Numerous requests for back copies of *The Observer* convinced me that 'Unquoted' deserved a prolonged shelf life. That is how this book came about.

Brian's articles each contained a wealth of advice on

specific subjects and, in view of this, we decided essentially to maintain the original character. Articles emerged as chapters and Brian embarked on a major updating exercise which encompassed the measures introduced in Chancellor Norman Lamont's 1991 Budget.

I would like to take this opportunity to thank Brian for his invaluable contributions to *The Observer* and for the immense amount of time and work which he has devoted to this project. My thanks, also, to my colleague, Sarah Whitebloom, who undertook much of the editing of this book.

It has been a pleasure to work with Brian — a man of many parts — over the years. He is acknowledged as one of the UK's foremost experts on small businesses: a factor which led to his secondment to Conservative Central Office in 1982–84 as an adviser on small-business policy. He is a past Master and current member of the Court of The Haberdashers Livery Company, a wine connoisseur and (so I am reliably informed) a formidable poker player.

As readers will discover, he is also a great authority on how to run a small business.

MELVYN MARCKUS
Editor: *Observer Business*

FOREWORD

It is a pleasure to have the opportunity to introduce this book, which brings together many of the articles which Brian Jenks has contributed over recent years to *The Observer*. The book provides a very useful overview of the day-to-day problems facing the would-be entrepreneur, as well as highlighting sources of help and advice. I am sure it will be welcomed by all those who are involved with small firms.

The Government is very proud of the part it has played in the spectacular growth of the small firms sector since 1979. There are now more small firms in Britain than ever before. This is most encouraging, and is of course mainly due to the enthusiasm and determination of the millions of people who have realised their ambition by starting and running their own business.

It was during the early 1980s that the Government took the necessary steps to ensure that the right conditions existed in Britain for enterprise to flourish – lower personal and corporate tax rates, the removal of unnecessary regulations and red tape, and appropriate advice and assistance to fledgling companies. The subsequent boom in the small firms sector has generated not only a very large number of new jobs and a significant contribution to national economic activity, but it has provided us with a broader based and more resilient economy.

The Government continues to regard the small firms sector as a priority area. As well as maintaining the framework I have outlined above, we are now moving one stage further by handing over responsibility for the delivery of enterprise support to the new network of Training and Enterprise Councils. These employer-led bodies, of which there are 82 in England and Wales, are ideally placed to assist new and growing companies in their locality. I am confident that by giving the reins to those who have direct experience of business life, we shall see yet more growth in the small firms sector in the coming decade.

ERIC FORTH
Small Firms Minister: Department of Employment

INTRODUCTION

In the New Year of 1990, when I started writing a series of articles for *The Observer*, on which this book is based, the outlook for business was reasonably buoyant. By the end of the year it had become apparent that the economy was in recession and this scenario has persisted during the first quarter of 1991 – reflected in a spate of bankruptcies, receiverships and liquidations.

The problems experienced by small and medium-sized enterprises and owner-managers have changed. The major objective in 1990 was to achieve higher sales in order to increase profits. Now, the emphasis is on cutting costs so that losses can be kept to a minimum and cash outflows contained.

This calls for a different style of management but, however depressing the outlook, owner-managers must not lose sight of the fact that, sooner or later, the recession will bottom out and trading conditions will improve. Not only will businesses recover; they will eventually flourish. So, the message is: Don't turn the heat off in the greenhouse if you want a prize-winning orchid.

The 'do's' and 'don'ts' for owner-managers during a recession include:

• Review your invoicing and debt-collecting procedures. The objective is to minimise the time between receiving a customer's order and crediting his cash to your bank account. There are several stages of which the first is a quick response to the request for goods or services. Next comes the prompt issue of an invoice – with no errors – making sure that the customer is fully aware of the date when payment is due. Then, as soon as the debt becomes overdue, hard chasing is cailed for.

• Review credit control procedures. This is a time when you

must be more careful than ever to check whether a prospective customer is going to pay his account as soon as it falls due. Bad debts will prove disastrous.

- Review your stock levels to ensure that you are not carrying more stock or work in progress than is necessary to fulfill orders which are likely to be running at a lower level than a year ago. There is no point in holding stocks of finished goods which you cannot sell.

- Review your staff. This is the time to run a lean business. Is a policy of natural wastage and no recruitment sufficient, or do you need to dismiss any staff who are not proving productive? Are there instances where early retirement should be encouraged?

- Review prices of goods and services. Are they competitive? Remember: a business which offers quality and delivers the goods at the right price can be expected to win orders at the expense of less efficient rivals.

- Review overheads. For example, could professional fees be reduced if more work was carried out in-house? Could car expenses be reduced by cutting back on the number of vehicles or the car models provided for directors and senior employees? Is there scope for reducing advertising and public relations costs, perhaps by switching from a large agency, with a penchant for large campaigns, to a small agency where you may receive better value for money? Could bank interest be reduced by careful monitoring of existing arrangements? Can cheques, for example, be banked more quickly? Or, if you deal in foreign currencies, can delays in transferring funds from abroad be reduced?

- In hard times, keep in close touch with your customers to ensure they pay your accounts as they become due. The same goes for your suppliers, in order to ensure that deliveries are maintained, even if you ask for a little longer to pay. Above all, stay in touch with your bank manager. He must have confidence in you and in the way you manage your business so that, if necessary, facilities can be increased to tide you over the bad times.

- Review your premises. Do you really require all the space you own or lease? It may not be the ideal time to move but it may prove beneficial to keep part of the premises empty in order to save on heating, lighting, etc. Is it possible to sub-let space on a temporary basis?

- Remember: sooner or later there will be an upturn so do not dismiss key staff who will be essential when trading improves.

- Don't close down operations which could provide future growth.

- Don't cut corners on procedures which may involve you in time-consuming arguments and possibly penalties. Make sure that VAT returns are submitted on time, accounts are prepared and copies submitted to Companies House within the time limits.

As I have already mentioned, management during a recession calls for a different style. The emphasis must be on planning while waiting for the tide to turn. This is a time when the owner-manager must satisfy himself that his business is viable. There is no point in persevering with a business which is not viable in the medium to long term. This is even more pertinent if the owner-manager has given personal guarantees in respect of bank overdrafts or leases.

Even if the business is viable, it may have to be acknowledged that profits will decline or disappear in the short term. This need not, in itself, give rise to panic. In times of adversity, management must not bury its head in the sand; on the contrary, it must be prepared to act that much more quickly. Pretending all is well will not help when:

- A supplier threatens to cut off goods or services, or sue you for non-payment.

- A customer has not paid on time and you are worried about his financial status.

- The bank manager wants to discuss the renewal of your overdraft facilities.

Today's manager must be prepared to be tough but he must also be fair. Five essentials are as follows:

- Watch the cash flow.

- Control the cheque book.

- Don't let routine procedures slip.

- Talk to colleagues, bankers, suppliers and customers.

- Be patient. Cycles come and go. The sun will shine again.

BRIAN JENKS
March 1991

START-UP

ARE YOU AN ENTREPRENEUR?

One of the principal reasons why so many businesses go bust lies in the fact that the founder is not cut out to start up and develop his own operation. Sometimes this is due to a lack of knowledge, skill or business experience; sometimes to personal weaknesses.

So let us attempt to analyse the character traits of an entrepreneur. Although entrepreneurs are a diverse species, there are clearly some common factors. Permit me to quote from *The British Entrepreneur*, a study prepared by accountants Ernst & Young and the Cranfield School of Management. 'Not all entrepreneurs are cast in the same mould. Indeed it would be an extremely dull world if they were. Almost by definition they defy categorisation.

'Some have a strong sense of humour, some none; some thrive on publicity and adulation, others are virtual hermits; some have an overwhelming need for power, others for creativity; some need the trappings of wealth, others lead very simple lives. Whatever the difference is, there is one factor which all successful entrepreneurs have in common − they and their firms are always on the move.'

It must be appreciated that management skills can be learned, whereas entrepreneurial ability is a matter of flair; either you have it or you don't. Business requires both skills, the flair of the entrepreneur and the solid competence of the manager.

It is dangerous to generalise but some of the characteristics of the entrepreneur, in contrast to the manager, are: belief in himself and his business; belief in wealth and material gain; and belief in delegation.

Entrepreneurial talent and management skills may not both be present in the one person. This may lead to the idea of partnership and, indeed, as the business flourishes and expands, the creation of a management team.

Your first step in the business world should be self-analysis. Do you possess the qualities to become an entrepreneur? The quiz may help you find this out.

Meanwhile, *The British Entrepreneur* encompasses the results of a survey of the views of owner-managers of the top 100 entrepreneurial firms in the UK. One of the questions asked was: 'What are the critical factors for success?' The answers came under three key headings:

Marketing

A unique product; an innovative approach; a good fundamental idea; aggressive sales and marketing strategies; active selling; quality; price; and heavy marketing investment.

Management

Dedicated senior management; hard work and commitment of staff; tight financial controls; cash flow; investment for the long term; regular reviews and overhaul of the management structure; disciplined and cost-effective management of employees; unwavering and total support from initial backers.

Personal

Vision; hard work; concentration; flexibility; persistence; and the ability to recognise opportunities.

The owner-managers were asked about their personal life and family background.

Many came from families where the father had some form of small firm or self-employment background while the mother cared for the home and family. It was interesting to note that not one was an only child and more than half came from families with more than two children.

The previous survey, in 1988, revealed that the group showed low educational attainments – 45 per cent left school at the age of 16 and few attained any further qualifications.

The 1989 list revealed somewhat greater academic attainments but apart from the obvious value of management skills which result from taking an MBA, few owner-managers saw any relationship between educational achievements and their current success.

There is a misconception that successful entrepreneurs fail several times before making the breakthrough. Not true. With this sample only 20 per cent had started-up more than one business.

The average age of the entrepreneurs when they started their first business was 32, the youngest being 24. Presumably they gained valuable skills and product knowledge between school and start-up. On the other hand, the majority started businesses which bore no commercial relationship to their previous employment.

All rather confusing. Perhaps we should dwell on the wisdom of Lord Hanson: 'We determined our objectives 21 years ago and the insistence on pursuing those objectives is the key to our success. The transition of small business to large combine can be done but you have to want to do it. It comes down to a matter of determination and hard work. Getting up before the others. Staying up later than the others.'

ARE YOU AN ENTREPRENEUR?

The crucial factor in a business – especially when it is just starting up – is the calibre of the person, or people, in charge.

A new business is, essentially, as good as the person who is masterminding the strategy. Too often the role of entrepreneur is confused with that of a manager. A business requires the skills of both, but it is of paramount importance that management ability is not confused with entrepreneurial skills. More to the point: a manager should not delude himself that he is an entrepreneur.

This quiz is designed to help you gain some idea of the extent of your potential.

---

1 Do you prefer to work on your own, with as little outside direction as possible?
   a) yes ☐
   b) usually ☐
   c) no ☐

2 Do you feel, given well-defined criteria and adequate resources, you will produce a favourable result?
   a) yes ☐
   b) usually ☐
   c) sometimes ☐

3 Do you find a limited working environment frustrating?
   a) yes ☐
   b) usually ☐
   c) can cope ☐

4 If something you are involved in goes wrong, do you feel personally responsible?
   a) yes ☐
   b) sometimes ☐
   c) no ☐

5 Do you suggest changes in operations which involve you?
   a) often ☐
   b) sometimes ☐
   c) seldom ☐

6 Do you enjoy working with other people?
   a) usually ☐
   b) sometimes ☐
   c) seldom ☐

7 Do you enjoy assessing risks and acting on your assessments?
   a) yes ☐
   b) sometimes ☐
   c) no ☐

8 Do you apply yourself equally to all tasks you face?
   a) yes ☐
   b) usually ☐
   c) no ☐

9 Are you content with your achievements to date?
   a) yes ☐
   b) generally ☐
   c) no ☐

10 Are you content with your present lifestyle?
   a) yes ☐
   b) generally ☐
   c) no ☐

11 Do you care what your friends and business associates think of you?
   a) yes ☐
   b) sometimes ☐
   c) no ☐

12 Do you have a clear idea of what you want to do over the next three years?
   a) yes ☐
   b) reasonably clear ☐
   c) no ☐

13 Do you think you have control over and can influence your future?
   a) yes ☐
   b) sometimes ☐
   c) no ☐

14 Do you put your failures behind you?
   a) yes ☐
   b) sometimes ☐
   c) no ☐

15 Are you outspoken – sometimes to your detriment – about what you think?
   a) yes ☐
   b) sometimes ☐
   c) no ☐

16 Do you believe you are adequately compensated for work you have done?
   a) yes ☐
   b) sometimes ☐
   c) no ☐

17 Do poor working conditions affect your performance?
   a) yes ☐
   b) sometimes ☐
   c) no ☐

18 Do your goals and aims have the support of your family and those close to you?
   a) yes ☐
   b) usually ☐
   c) no ☐

19 What level of growth potential do you think the free enterprise system has?
   a) unlimited ☐
   b) limited ☐
   c) very little ☐

20 If the situation is not conducive to your plans, do you:
a) Carry on regardless? ☐
b) Wait for it to improve? ☐
c) Adjust your plans? ☐

ARE YOU AN ENTREPRENEUR?

1: a = 3, b = 2, c = 1; 2: a = 3, b = 2, c = 1; 3: a = 3, b = 2, c = 1;
4: a = 3, b = 2, c = 1; 5: a = 3, b = 2, c = 1; 6: a = 1, b = 2, c = 3;
7: a = 3, b = 2, c = 1; 8: a = 1, b = 2, c = 3; 9: a = 1, b = 2, c = 3;
10: a = 1, b = 2, c = 1; 11: a = 3, b = 2, c = 1; 12: a = 3, b = 2, c = 1;
13: a = 3, b = 2, c = 1; 14: a = 1, b = 2, c = 3; 15: a = 3, b = 2, c = 1;
16: a = 1, b = 2, c = 3; 17: a = 1, b = 2, c = 3; 18: a = 3, b = 2, c = 1;
19: a = 3, b = 2, c = 1; 20: a = 2, b = 1, c = 3.

Rating yourself:

Over 55: You probably know exactly what you intend to do – if you have not already started. And the chances are that you did not need the confirmation of this quiz to reassure you about your entrepreneurial drive. But since you appear to have the motivation and attitudes to succeed, make sure you seek out expert advice before you go any further.

50 to 55: You are on your way. A full profile of your personality would probably place you firmly in the 'likely to succeed' category.

45 to 50: The ability, the motivation and the attitudes to win through is probably there. But there is also the possibility of a lack of commitment in some areas. Perhaps family responsibilities give rise to caution; perhaps you are not committed to the accumulation of wealth. More likely, you are already in a job and, not being an intending entrepreneur, lack the clarity of goals.

40 to 45: Definite need for close reappraisal if you are intending to launch yourself forth as an entrepreneur. Perhaps your skills are more management-oriented? Or perhaps a cooperative or partnership would be more suitable?

Below 40: A decided scepticism, even lack of belief in the system, is indicated here. You may be highly skilled, but are perhaps unwilling – or unable – to do battle as a business entrepreneur.

HOW GORDON FAILED

Not long ago, Gordon, an old aquaintance of mine, dropped into my office. I was immediately struck by the change in his appearance; he looked generally unkempt, his face was drawn and he appeared to have developed a limp. I remembered him as a moderately successful director of a building contracting business: slightly impetuous but with some good ideas. I asked, with some foreboding, how life was treating him.

It appeared that Gordon's problems began some 18 months ago when he took early retirement in order to start up a garden centre with his wife, Alice, a keen horticulturalist. He commuted part of his pension, took out a second mortgage on his house and used the proceeds to install a glasshouse and a wooden building on the paddock which adjoins his garden.

According to Gordon, business had gone very well at first. Sales amounted to £1000 in the first week alone and more than £5000 for the first month. His policy had been to mark-up plants and other products by 100 per cent – a practice which, he assumed, would yield a good profit.

But then things started to go wrong. Gordon had spent almost £10,000 on stock – including some exotic species of particular interest to Alice. Alas, in the wake of last summer's drought, Gordon found that his water supply was inadequate.

Gordon's woes were far from over. Storms damaged his glasshouse and wreaked havoc on the exotic plants. To his dismay he found that he was not adequately insured.

I then learned of Gordon's battle with the local council which arose, so it would seem, because he had not received the necessary planning permission for the garden-centre building.

In the event, sales failed to expand after the initial flurry of demand and turnover totalled a little less than £30,000 for the year.

Not that Gordon's problems ended there. He had also fallen foul of Customs and Excise, because he had not registered for VAT.

And, when he completed the Employer's Annual Statement, Gordon discovered he was also in default with the Inland Revenue because he had not operated PAYE income tax in respect of his part-time employees.

His bank manager, having agreed one increase in his overdraft, was not prepared to advance further funds – a factor which had driven Gordon, in a state of panic, to my office.

The limp was explained by the fact that, while moving bags of peat, he had injured his back.

It took Gordon the best part of an hour to impress upon me how hard he and Alice had worked, how they had been unable to take a holiday, how there had been angry telephone calls from customers; all of which led to family quarrels. He and Alice now faced the prospect of losing money, and possibly their house, unless some arrangement could be reached with the bank.

Gordon's tale is a classic example of starting a business without thinking the project through and making a plan. So what could I do to help?

Clearly, the VAT and PAYE problems could be resolved, although Customs and Excise and the Inland Revenue would require payment. As for Gordon's ability to raise further funds, I was not particularly optimistic.

Bearing in mind the fact that his business had already lost substantial sums, could Gordon show that he would fare any better in the future?

I anticipated that there would be some income-tax rebate in respect of trading losses to date, but accounts would have to be prepared in order to make the claim. A substantial part of any such income-tax recovery would be needed to pay Customs and Excise and the Revenue along with other creditors.

It seemed to me that Gordon and Alice's best hope would be to take a partner who might be prepared to back them if a business plan indicated that the operation could be viable.

If Gordon could not find a suitable partner, he would have

to consider going back to work: perhaps as an employee in a somewhat more successful garden centre.

It is easy to be wise after the event and lecture Gordon as to what he should have done, but others may learn useful lessons from his mishaps.

When Gordon first decided to start up a garden centre, he should have thought the project through carefully.

He should have considered what would be distinctive about his centre that would attract customers to him rather than his rivals. How many customers could he expect? How much would they spend? Was the location suitable?

In terms of finance he should have worked out what the capital costs would be. Would sales yield sufficient profit to cover running costs and provide a reasonable remuneration for Alice and himself? Who would deal with administrative details such as VAT and PAYE and keep the records?

Gordon should have prepared an outline plan in order to satisfy himself that the proposal was viable. He should have discussed it with his business friends, his accountant and his bank manager. Most important of all, he should have asked himself whether he and Alice were really cut out to run their own business.

Further, did Gordon or Alice possess sufficient technical knowledge? Did they have the relevant business experience? Could he organise and motivate others? Did he have the commitment and perserverance to see the business through bad times as well as good?

If he had been satisfied in respect of all these factors, he should have gone on to prepare a more detailed business plan in order to:

- Determine his objectives.

- Identify his strategies.

- Specify profit forecasts and cash requirements.

Gordon should not have gone beyond this point without taking advice. He should have consulted his accountant, his bank manager, a chartered surveyor and perhaps the local enterprise agency.

If he had taken such steps he would have known whether the business proposal stood a serious chance of success; or he might have heeded the warning signals and decided not to risk his money and retirement security.

The lessons are simple:

- You must plan your business before you start.

- You must be satisfied that you are capable of running such a business.

- You must take advice.

HOW JEREMY SUCCEEDED

Despite spiralling liquidations, reflecting the impact of the recession (and not a little mismanagement), it is worth remembering that some businesses are thriving and many new businesses are still being formed.

The UK has always enjoyed a reputation for innovation and one only has to meet the winners of the Department of Trade and Industry's Small Firms' Merit Awards for Research and Technology to realise how much talent is on tap.

It was my privilege to be part of such a success story. In 1986 a young man called Jeremy Hill visited California and noticed that the cold cabinets in the supermarkets had screens in front of them to prevent the cold air escaping. The screens were made of PVC strips which the customer could see through but which did not prevent him from putting his hand into the cabinet to take out dairy products, cheese, cold meats, etc.

Jeremy quickly became convinced that this was a good idea. In 1986 the major benefit from installing chiller strips was the saving in power. Hygiene and temperature control had yet to become major issues.

So convinced was Jeremy that, upon his return to England, he gave up his job and joined a colleague in a business venture to market the product. First time round he did not succeed, probably because the business was short of capital and was unable to convey the benefits of the product to sufficient customers.

But Jeremy kept faith and it was not long before he and his wife, Sue, formed a new company based on virtually the same product – albeit somewhat wiser as a result of the initial failure. If at first you don't succeed. . .

It was hard work. Jeremy and Sue assembled the chiller strip blinds in the garage, working seven days a week. Jeremy visited customers to fit the blinds and, at the same time, searched for new customers. What drove them was the conviction that they had found a niche, a product which was topical and where competition was minimal. Help came in 1989 by way of a change in attitudes towards food hygiene. Outbreaks of salmonella and Edwina Currie's egg warnings served to focus retailers' minds. Customers would no longer tolerate the sight of melting packs of butter. Action was called for and legislation, which became effective on 1 April 1991, requires most dairy products to be stored in conditions which ensure a product temperature of 8°C or less. The fact that 1989 and 1990 were hot summers reinforced the case for keeping dairy products in cool conditions which, nonetheless, would attract customers. Shops and supermarkets which installed chiller strips were able to make significant savings on electricity costs.

Jeremy decided to submit chiller strip blinds to the British Standards Institution for testing. The £5000 outlay represented a significant item of expenditure but a satisfactory result provided all the proof needed that chiller strips worked, temperatures were kept down to required levels, and major power savings were to be had. This endorsement was highlighted in brochures and sales literature. Tests carried out by the Institute of Food Research on behalf of the Ministry of Agriculture provided further proof that chiller blinds offered a relatively inexpensive method of temperature control.

Jeremy and Sue's business duly expanded. They worked on the basis that you should not turn any order away, as long as you were satisfied that the customer would pay the bill. This sometimes meant sending the chiller blinds to customers with fitting instructions, rather than delivering the product themselves.

Slowly, Jeremy and Sue built up their staff. They invited the sales manager, Ken Patel, to become a director and shareholder and take on a national role. Teams of assemblers and fitters were created and extra sales staff taken on. A bonus scheme was introduced for staff – the result being that Jeremy and Sue employ a keen workforce who support the business 100 per cent.

Sue was responsible for book-keeping, invoicing and office

administration. Not surprisingly, she was overwhelmed, but although invoicing and debt collection fell behind, she remained in control and key tasks such as VAT returns were kept up to date.

By the spring of 1990, Jeremy and Sue realised they could no longer operate from a garage in the suburbs of London. In the event, they alighted on an agricultural building which could be converted to light industrial use in Cambridgeshire, along with a four-bedroomed house to accommodate them and their newly arrived baby. Here they discovered that good-quality staff could be taken on at significantly lower rates of pay than in the outskirts of London.

On occasions, it was necessary to beat off poachers. Would-be rivals attempted to use extracts and photographs from Jeremy's brochures but solicitors acted promptly to stop such infringements.

There is room for expansion in the new premises and Jeremy believes he could produce as many as 1000 blinds per week. With 500,000 shops in this country selling food, and half of these suitable candidates for chiller-screen treatment, there should be no shortage of customers. Jeremy has now taken on an in-house accountant and is preparing to export to mainland Europe. The EC may well follow suit and introduce legislation requiring dairy products to be stored at a temperature similar or perhaps lower than in the UK. Meanwhile, Jeremy already has a new product in mind to enable the business to diversify from merely selling chiller strips.

The last time Jeremy visited me he stressed that all this was exceedingly hard work and he did not want to continue at the same pace indefinitely. So he is beginning to look to the future. Turnover this year will probably be in the region of £1.5 million so Jeremy, Sue and the sales director have an investment of real value.

Looking back I can see that Jeremy and Sue made some mistakes, but they were right about the majority of things. This could be seen as a model start-up. In the first place, Jeremy was the right person. He had the commitment and knowledge of the product and market. He perceived that there was a niche for his product. Chiller strips could be sold on the basis of power-saving, food-temperature-control requirements and the improved appearance of products stored in cabinets with such strips. Certainly, Edwina Currie and two hot summers helped.

Jeremy realised that there was a large market for his chiller strips and little competition. In these circumstances it was essential that the quality of his product and service was good; he did not have to compete on price.

Jeremy and Sue made it a priority to employ well-motivated staff and apart from the bonus scheme they have encouraged employees to go on training courses organised by Leadership Development.

They have never turned away orders and have made it a priority to keep customers happy.

They may have fallen down somewhat on credit control, invoicing, debt collection and bank arrangements but they have not been too concerned about this because their priorities have been to look after the product, the people working for them and their customers.

They have not stood still with one product and one market, and they are looking to expand into Europe and introduce a second product. At the same time they will strengthen their management team and make sure they have proper information on which to base decisions.

Finance has not proved a problem so far because the business has enjoyed a very positive cash flow. In view of the track record, there should be little difficulty in obtaining bank facilities or investor participation, if required, during the next stage of expansion.

Perhaps this true story will encourage those who have a good business idea and perceive a market for it.

PARTNERSHIP OR COMPANY?

PARTNERSHIPS

Partnerships are a popular way of structuring a business enterprise for three key reasons:

- Start-ups may wish to avoid excessive complication or formality in their affairs and a partnership is often the most suitable option.

- There are usually tax advantages to partnerships, particularly in the early stages when profits may be relatively small or non-existent.

- The business or profession (such as solicitors or accountants) may be required, by a regulatory body, to operate as a partnership.

There are, however, certain disadvantages to partnerships, the most significant being the fact that a partner's liability is unlimited. This means that if the business incurs losses or suffers large claims, the individual partner may be required to fund such losses from personal assets, including his house.

Partnerships tend to enjoy a somewhat lower profile than limited companies. This can prove beneficial in certain circumstances: there are no shares to be valued and there is no requirement to file accounts or publish details of profits and partners' earnings. On the other hand, partnerships may find it more difficult to raise funds from banks and other financial institutions.

A less obvious disadvantage is that partnerships often lack the clear-cut management structure of a limited company. It may be that responsibilities for finance, marketing and personnel are not clearly defined within a partnership but rather that each partner assumes he can have a say in, and take a degree of responsibility for, all aspects of the firm's management.

This can lead to differences of opinion between partners, decisions may prove difficult to reach and there is no clear mandate as to who should implement them.

Partners, particularly in smaller firms, may be reluctant to give up their direct involvement in the management of the firm's affairs. And, unless they have been consulted in advance, they may be unwilling to accept decisions and advice made by another partner.

In these circumstances, partnerships, perhaps above all, can benefit from professional advice. Major firms of accountants (invariably partnerships themselves) are particularly well placed to carry out such reviews.

Many of the requirements for the efficient running of a partnership are the same as those for any other business. Here are some points to consider when reviewing the organisation and structure of a partnership.

Leadership

When the partnership has reached a certain size, it is no longer feasible to have all the partners sitting round a table making decisions on the basis of a consensus view. It must be decided who is responsible for what.

- A procedure must be agreed for selecting a leader or managing partner and this must be understood and accepted by all concerned.

- Partners must calculate how much time they ought to spend on managing the firm. For some, this may be none at all. But in large firms the leaders may find themselves devoting virtually all their time to managing the business, rather than focusing on earning profits.

Strategy

In a small business, it is difficult to set aside enough time for making policy decisions about the future of the firm — customers and clients are demanding.

- It is therefore necessary to have a plan, perhaps a five-year plan, to set out what the partnership hopes to achieve, in practical as well as financial terms.

- You must decide which areas of the business should be developed and where additional services can be provided.

- You should consider whether the firm's objectives might be best served by merging your business with another, one that can provide skills or market opportunities not currently available to you. You should also consider whether there is a case for incorporation (if that is permitted for your type of business or profession).

- Your strategy should be used as a basis for developing a business plan and setting financial targets against which performance can be measured.

Business development

Can you survive and flourish in a more competitive marketplace? You will need to:

- Allocate specific responsibility for business development and marketing to one or more partners. Make sure that enough time is allocated to partners to attract new clients. Work out how your business can be distinguished from its competitors. This will involve reviewing your products or services and the prices charged.

- Consider the case for advertising and agree on what forms of marketing activity or public relations are most appropriate for your business.

Resources

Resources relate to people as well as money. Do you have trouble finding and keeping high-quality staff?

- Make sure you provide training and a means of developing skills – including those of your partners.

- Ensure that you can offer attractive career opportunities to capable employees of all ages.

- Consider your staff-appraisal techniques and make sure there are established criteria for promotion and admission to partnership.

Management information

In order to make plans, manage the business and reach informed decisions, you need accurate information.

- The first essential is to prepare budgets in order to assess performance.

- A service business, such as a professional firm, needs to set in place adequate systems for recording time spent by partners and staff.

- You should know which of your activities are the most profitable.

- You need to consider whether you are making sufficient use of information technology, computers, word processors and fax machines.

Cash

In these times of weak cash flow, it is vital that time and materials are converted into invoices, and invoices into cash, as soon as possible.

- Review procedures for billing and collecting cash from clients or customers.

- Take account of the amounts of cash that partners draw out to maintain themselves and their families.

- Consider the method of financing the partnership: is there a case for having partners subscribe more capital to enable the business to run on a smaller bank overdraft?

Taxation

The objective is to minimise the partnership's tax burden:

- Consider whether a partnership is necessarily the correct structure – particularly if the business and profits have grown to a point where they exceed partners' remuneration requirements.

- Review borrowing arrangements to make sure that interest qualifies for income-tax relief from the earliest possible date.

- Pension arrangements are important for the self-employed; you should check that they are efficient and relevant to your needs.

- Ensure that the arrangements for ownership of business premises and property are tax-effective.

- Check whether a change of accounting date might produce tax savings.

- Make sure that partnership appointments are timed to achieve maximum tax benefit.

Much of the above is relevant to the smallest partnership – from the husband and wife team running a farm to the mother and daughter boutique venture. It is essential to medium-sized partnerships, involving perhaps six or more partners, a great many of which relate to the professions.

Most are profitable but many are not as profitable as they would be – if they were better managed.

The Limited Way to Enjoy Your Own Company

A business start-up can operate as a company, a partnership or a sole proprietorship – whichever is most appropriate. Even if a business does not start as a formal company, the proprietor is likely to apply for company status once a reasonable level of profitability has been achieved.

Business incorporation means legally forming or acquiring a company – a process with which not all businessmen are familiar.

When incorporating, the majority of small-business owners choose private limited company status, which leaves the option open to convert to a public limited company at a later date.

The formation of a company is best handled by a professional – usually an accountant, solicitor or registration agent. Although it is possible to form your own tailor-made company, the process can be expensive. The more common practice is to acquire a 'ready-made' or 'off-the-shelf' company, which is available for immediate use and can be restructured to specific requirements.

It may be necessary to change an off-the-shelf company's name to a more appropriate title. It is essential to ensure that the chosen name is available, is not too similar to that of an existing company and does not risk misinterpretation. A professional adviser should be able to check on this within a matter of hours.

In approximate terms some £800 should cover the essential steps needed to put a company on the road:

- Purchase of an off-the-shelf company.

- Alteration of its name and articles to suit individual needs.

- Issue or transfer of initial subscribers' shares.

- Appointment of directors and a company secretary.

Bear in mind that any complications will, inevitably, increase the cost.

Every company has two principle constitutional documents: the Memorandum of Association and the Articles of Association. The Memorandum defines the company's objectives, states the amount of capital and confirms limited liability, while the Articles contain the company's internal regulations. In practice, the Articles follow closely the specimens in the Schedules to the Companies Act.

Recent legislation has paved the way for what is known as a 'General Commercial Company' with general short-form objectives. However, additional clauses may have to be added to clarify such matters as borrowing powers and the establishment of pension schemes.

Copies of the constitutional documents are deposited at Companies House, along with a statement of share capital, details in respect of the directors and secretary and the registered office.

All companies must have at least two shareholders, individuals or corporate bodies, who may act as beneficial owners or through nominees.

The initial amount of issued share capital will depend on the nature of the business and its capital requirements. Professional advisers will be able to recommend the scale of capitalisation, and many private start-ups begin with as little as £100 fixed capital. Additional funds may be injected later.

All private companies must have at least one director and a company secretary; a sole director cannot act as secretary.

When company ownership is equally divided between proprietor directors and outside shareholders it is advisable to establish, at an early stage, a mechanism for resolving disputes. Deadlocks between proprietors and directors can prove exceedingly damaging.

A company cannot begin to trade until the Certificate of Incorporation is issued and directors are appointed.

A company's registered office is its legal address where documents can be served and is the factor which usually decides the company's tax district. For this reason many small companies use their accountant's address as their registered office. The company name must be conspicuously displayed outside places of business.

Registration of a company for VAT purposes is made through local Customs and Excise Offices, while an employees' PAYE scheme is set up by application to a local Inspector of Taxes.

When making arrangements for banking facilities, a bank manager will require a corporate mandate form with specimen signatures and sight of the Memorandum and Articles of Association, the Certificate of Incorporation and any Certificate of Change of Name.

An early task for a newly incorporated company is to arrange stationery supplies. The Companies Act 1985 and European Communities Act stipulate certain details for inclusion on letterheads. These are: the full corporate name (including the word 'limited'), the company registration number, the country of incorporation and the registered office address. If appropriate, invoices and statements must also state the VAT registration number.

If a company uses an abbreviated or trading name and a trading address, such details should be given at the foot of the page. All other information is optional.

Corporate management is vested in the board of directors. Large boards usually appoint a chairman and a managing director with specified roles. Numerous statutory provisions supplement the Articles of Association and it is imperative that all directors understand their duties, responsibilities and liabilities.

It is the company secretary's duty to ensure the proper maintenance of the minute book, the register of directors and shareholders, and any mortgages or charges against the company. He should also have custody of, and record the use of, the company seal.

Every company should select and register a date on which its statutory accounts will be prepared (Accounting Reference Date). Because such accounts must be audited the board should appoint qualified auditors at an early stage. The auditors can give advice and assist with many of the required post-incorporation formalities.

Once a company has been formed, there are certain responsibilities. Each year, accounts must be prepared and audited, and an Annual Return filed which details shareholders, directors, and the company secretary. If there are any changes of directors or secretary during the year, a return must be made so that the company's file is up to date.

No one should become a director of a company without being fully aware of the consequences. The risks may just prove greater than the rewards.

PLANNING FOR SUCCESS

THINK BEFORE YOU LEAP

Spring is here and the sun is shining. As someone once said: 'Who can think of dying on a day like this?'

The economic outlook is not favourable: interest rates are high and competition as keen as ever; but there are still entrepreneurs eager to start up in business, many for the first time.

So how does it happen? What are the first things to do? Obviously, you must decide what sort of business suits you best. Should it be manufacturing which requires heavy investment in plant and stock? Should it be wholesaling or retailing? Where have all the window cleaners gone? Perhaps your village is short of a hardware shop, or a service, or a financial consultant. Not much capital cost involved here, but are you sure people will want to consult you? Perhaps a franchise is the answer? Exploit someone else's idea to limit your costs – and possibly your profits as well.

Or are you going to be rather more methodical and peruse the index of a careers book (abattoirs, accountancy, advertising. . .) ticking off those which are plausible.

In practice, businesses do not usually start this way. More likely the prospective entrepreneur will perceive a gap, some process, product or service which is not available or is not being carried out efficiently and will say: 'I could do that' or 'I could do better than that.'

Most of us have such ideas: why, for example, can't the tops of orange juice cartons be designed to open and pour more easily?

The majority of us note such shortcomings but, other than complain, do nothing about it. By way of contrast, the entrepreneur notes the shortcoming and considers whether this presents him with a business opportunity. In practice, he will identify opportunities in an area of business or service with which he is already familiar.

But before going any further, you must ascertain whether you are qualified to run your own business. In short, do you possess the technical knowledge and the relevant business experience? Have you the ability to organise and motivate others? Have you the commitment and perseverance to see the business through in bad times as well as good? Above all, are you prepared to work all hours of the day – and perhaps the night – in pursuit of your ambition? If not, beware of starting at all. If you are satisfied that you are fully committed, you should proceed with your plans.

At this stage, planning does not need to be sophisticated but it is essential, no matter how modest your business venture. Remember: it is too late to start planning after you have discovered problems and depleted your capital. Planning is essential in terms of:

- Discipline – planning helps you organise your thoughts, challenge traditional ideas and create the climate for new ones.

- Direction – it serves to communicate a positive 'top down' management style which will help convince others such as employees, investors and bankers of the direction you believe the business should take.

- Control – a benchmark is established against which to monitor the day-to-day decision-making process.

The basic steps in planning your business are:

Objectives

Why are you in business? How rich do you wish to be? Many businessmen never ask themselves such questions, let alone answer them. Decide what you want. Is it profit, security of investment, employment, influence or a stimulating working environment?

Set a profit target. Most businessmen want to make a profit, but how much profit? Strongly managed businesses decide on a profit target and then create budgets to achieve that target. Record your objectives.

Strategies

Write a brief statement covering alternative actions which the business could take to achieve the objectives and profit target. Analyse the environment in which your business will operate – i.e. the economic, legal and tecnological factors. Analyse your business. Review your products, administration, staff, finance and marketing. Identify constraints, which may be economic, legal or moral or relate to such matters as union influence. Analyse possible courses of action in the light of such constraints and decide which strategies are the best to adopt.

Evaluation

This ground work will have been undertaken by you alone, although you will presumably have found it useful to discuss your ideas with business acquaintances along with your accountant and bank manager.

You have now reached the point where you should be able to assess whether your business idea is a starter and whether you are the person to exploit it. Should the answer be 'no', then you should not embark on such a venture, although you might explore the possibility of a partnership or the sale of your idea.

If you are satisfied that the project is viable, the next stage is to prepare a more formal business plan and take advice from your accountant (a priority), your bank manager, your solicitor and the Local Enterprise Agency.

A business plan should cover such specifics as: the product, process or service; finance; organisation and administration; and employees and marketing. A considerable amount of literature is available (see appendix) but it is important to bear in mind that despite the wealth of advice, this is your business plan and you should write it.

BLUEPRINT FOR A BUSINESS

Having convinced yourself that your business idea is feasible, the time has come to prepare a detailed business plan. This will:

- Put flesh on the bones of your business idea so that you can be satisfied that your theories will work in practice.

- Provide you with a selling document to attract investment, either in the shape of bank loans or venture capital, or perhaps a government grant.

- Serve as a blueprint for the future management of your business against which achievements can be monitored and management decisions made.

Remember that some 60 out of 100 plans are rejected out of hand. This means that your plan must be factual yet attractive. It must emphasise the plus points of your business but not disguise the risks and it should explain how you propose to overcome or minimise such risks.

I would advise the following headings:

Summary

The business plan should open with a concise overview of your plan. It should describe you, your business idea, what is exceptional about it, what you require by way of investment, what profit an investor may expect and what you have put into the business yourself. Be warned: many will read no further than the summary unless you whet their appetite.

Background

A brief history of the business, highlighting significant successes, details of present financing, shareholders and business partners.

Product

A layman's description of the product or service what it is and how it is used. Also explain the advantages of your product. Is it cheaper? Is it better quality? What unique features does it possess? Is it still in the research and development stage or has it been patented? What is the projected life span of the product or service? What new products are competitors likely to introduce? What is the profitability of each product or service? The credibility of your sales forecast often depends on the investor's perception of your product or service.

Management and personnel

Include this section immediately after your summary. Many investors take the view that it is better to back good management with a bad product than a good product with bad management.

Communicate the capabilities of yourself and your management team; demonstrate that you have the technical skills and relevant experience to enable you to succeed. Detailed curricula vitae as well as an organisation chart should appear as an appendix, but this section of your plan should include a summary of key managers, illustrating their roles, age, experience and expertise. If you have not yet filled all the management positions, make this clear and state your intentions.

Markets and marketing

Sales figures are difficult to forecast with any accuracy and, therefore, are the most important to justify. You must show that you understand your market and your position in it.

An investor will want to know whether your business is ahead of its competitors and whether it can maintain that lead. You must describe your market, its prospects and define your niche in that market in terms of product, territories and customers. You should include statistics and market research to support your findings.

Define your customers. Who are they, where are they, why will they buy from you? What is the competition, how powerful is it, how much of the market does it enjoy, what is its potential, how and why will you compete successfully and what will be the reaction to your entry into the market?

As for marketing, state your territorial objectives. Do you plan to export to the European Community? What is your pricing policy? What are your proposals in respect of advertising and public relations? Will you use your own sales force, distributors or agents?

You must show that there is a market demand for your product or service; that you understand your customers' needs and that the product meets such needs.

Manufacturing or service process

Describe how you produce your product or service, the availability of materials and labour, the advantages you have over competitors and your quality control procedures.

Include details of premises and facilities, current capacity and any expansion plans.

Financial information

Financial forecasts normally cover a three-year period and should consist of:

- Profit and loss accounts.

- Cash-flow statements.

- Pro-forma balance sheets.

- Statements of assumptions underlying your forecasts.

Such information is best included as an appendix but this section should include a summary and comments. The summary should embrace sales, gross profit margins, pre-tax profits, retained earnings and cash generated and expended for each of the three years.

The commentary should explain any initial losses incurred by the project and the transition into profit. You should draw attention to the maximum financial requirement – the low point in the cash-flow forecast – and highlight key assumptions. These should be justified by reference to other sections of the business plan: the sales forecast, for example, should be clearly justifiable by reference to the section on markets and marketing.

The preparation of forecasts is crucial. How many products will be sold and when? At what price? When will customers pay?

Answer such questions on the basis of the assumptions already set out. Then adopt a similar thought process to plan your production levels, costs and overheads. Forecasts for the first year should be set out on a month-by-month basis; subsequently it should suffice to work on a quarterly or perhaps even annual basis.

Do not undersell yourself. Investors may well choose to discount your forecasts. Some will start by halving the sales forecast, while doubling the time predicted to achieve full production. So don't be unduly conservative.

A sensitivity analysis may help you arrive at a realistic forecast. This involves the preparation of separate forecasts: on a 'realistic' basis and on a 'conservative' basis using different assumptions. Ask a series of 'what if' questions to demonstrate, for example, the impact of a 10 per cent reduction in sales or the effect of a three-month delay in the introduction of a new product.

Show all figures at current prices and make this clear in your assumptions. State how much funding you need and when it will be required including any further requirements.

Give a broad outline of the type of finance you are seeking such as ordinary share capital or a loan. You should also detail how an investor can realise his investment, when loans will be repaid and whether there will be an opportunity to realise shares.

Risks and rewards

Highlighting risks will add credibility to your business plan. It will indicate that you have perceived the risks and worked out how to overcome, or at least minimise, them. As an investor once remarked to me: 'Although I expect to run risks when I invest, I also expect to know what the risks are.' This is where a sensitivity analysis proves its worth. Compare best and worst scenarios, albeit not to the point of portraying a gloom and doom scenario.

Instead, consider a 'SWOT' analysis. Go through your Strengths, Weaknesses, Opportunities and Threats. And, as part of the 'opportunities' section, include the potential rewards to an investor if the plan is achieved.

Show what the company should be worth in three years and what this would represent in terms of the return on the investment.

Finally, a few practical hints on the preparation of a business plan:

- The business plan should not be too long or repetitive.

- Take advice, particularly from your accountant. He will be able to help you with the preparation of forecasts and financial information and it is advisable that he reviews the plan for technical content. But always remember, it is your plan and you should carry out the spade work.

- Plan the plan. Work out your section headings, decide what outside information you require, decide who is to coordinate the information and put the plan together. Include an index, the author's name and the date of compilation.

- Finally, try to make the plan look attractive, albeit not too extravagant, to the reader. The trick is to make him want to look inside.

CASH FLOW IS KING

It is abundantly clear that small businesses face a tough time in 1991 and beyond. Costs have risen and have yet to stabilise, while prospects for higher output and sales are far from encouraging. Against such a background, it is imperative for entrepreneurs to review the viability of their business. Finance, or to be more specific, cash, is the crucial factor.

With this in mind owner/managers should consider the following points:

- Do you have a cash-flow forecast for your business?

- Do you monitor the forecast regularly?

- Have you revised the forecast to take account of the latest information in respect of interest, business rates and the downturn in the economy?

- Are you satisfied that you will not need additional resources?

Unless you can answer 'yes' to all four questions you will almost certainly face problems in the current clime. Business management is much more difficult during a recession. Now is not the time to emulate an ostrich. Now is the time to act.

Face up to realities and prepare a cash-flow forecast month-by-month for the next 12 months. Is your cash flow positive – i.e. more receipts than payments? If it is, all well and good, but consider the second and third points above.

You must take into account the effects of inflation. If you are budgeting for higher sales prices you must recognise that most expenses will be higher too – especially salaries and services.

If cash flow is negative you may require additional finance, either by way of an injection of capital or, more likely, further bank facilities. Should this prove to be the case, the sooner the bank manager understands your situation and requirements, the better for both of you. Communication reduces stress.

It is important to understand the reasons for a negative cash flow, particularly as to whether this is a temporary or permanent state of affairs.

Temporary

• Outflow due to capital expenditure.

• One-off revenue expenditure on the development or marketing of a new product.

• Normal expenditure which creates a temporary dip in cash balances, e.g. taxation, dividends or directors' bonuses.

• Financing higher levels of stock or debtors which can be expected to drop after, for example, a period of high sales over the Christmas period (with the possible exception of last year).

Permanent

• Higher interest rates.

• Business rates which, in many instances, have exceeded general rates.

• An overall increase in costs which rise in line with the Retail Prices Index – i.e. salaries and most overheads.

• A downturn in sales due to reduced demand for products or services, or lower prices which may be necessary to compete effectively.

Temporary deteriorations in cash balances may correct themselves but nevertheless must be monitored. By way of example, capital expenditure might have to be delayed or funded through hire purchase or leasing. An advertising programme might have to be cancelled, postponed or cut back.

Any permanent downturn needs to be analysed to see whether the situation can be reversed or converted into a temporary variance.

This is when costs must be reviewed to detect whether savings can be made:

Can interest charges be cut by:

- Swifter invoicing?

- More efficient cash collection and banking?

- Reduction of stock levels?

- Delaying payments to creditors?

- Can the cost of premises be reduced by using less space or moving to an area where rents and business rates are lower?

- Can the workforce be reduced – perhaps by not replacing staff – without damage to the essential, albeit possibly reduced, business activity?

- Can sales be increased by expanding into new areas – such as Europe – or developing new products?

- Can margins be increased by charging higher prices or cutting discounts? The effect of higher prices on sales volume requires careful consideration.

If, having carried out such a review, there appears to be little prospect of converting a negative cash flow into a positive one, the owner/manager must answer a crucial question. Is he prepared to endure a limited period of negative cash flow on the assumption of an about-turn in circumstances which will leave him with a viable business?

Or should he consider a sale or closure before substantial losses are incurred?

Be prepared to take advice. It is at such times that accountants or business advisers can be of considerable assistance. Nor should you forget to make an early appointment with your bank manager.

GOOD HOUSEKEEPING

Any small business which increased its turnover by five per cent might, at first glance, appear to be doing rather well (particularly in the current climate). But, of course, with inflation running at close on ten per cent the opposite would be the case: unless the gross profit percentage had been maintained and overheads contained.

The Government, much to the business community's dismay, has relied on high interest rates to reduce consumer demand. The economic downturn resulting from this policy means that many small firms have experienced little, or no, increase in sales, while costs, unless controlled and reduced, have risen by at least as much as inflation.

It is essential, therefore, to review costs, particularly overheads, in order to see if there is any scope for savings.

Such a review should comprise two aspects:

- Good housekeeping: the basic requirement of any efficient business.

- A thorough analysis of the organisation of the business in order to eliminate non-productive (or not sufficiently productive) overheads.

Good housekeeping should include:

- Reduction of waste.

- Maintenance of lower stock levels.

- Reduction in the quality and capacity of company cars.

- Alternative quotations for goods and services.

- Controlled use of telephone, fax and messengers.

- More efficient power use, etc.

A strict cash control system is, of course, essential. Forecasts should be prepared and monitored regularly. It is useful to have in mind the amount of sales required to cover each £100 worth of overheads.

But, good housekeeping combined with careful monitoring may not be enough to keep a business out of difficulty. From time to time even successful businesses must radically review operations. Such a review can lead to a substantial reduction in overheads. This does not necessarily herald inferior services, in fact, service levels may well improve.

Paul Fuller, a colleague of mine at Touche Ross, has developed a procedure of Overhead Value Analysis (OVA). This consists of:

- Identification of activities, their products and costs.

- Establishment of the product's value to users.

- Joint consideration of activities by managers, users and consultants.

- Development of the most effective and practical organisation structures to meet business objectives.

- Production of an action plan for implementation.

First, it is necessary to establish the business objectives, then to analyse and organise the activities into activity centres and attribute costs to each.

Next, the user should assess the value of services and match the value against cost in order to reach conclusions along the following lines:

- High cost/low benefit: what is the effect/cost of reduction to nil (stopping the activity altogether)? Are there lower operating cost methods? How could benefits be increased?

- Low cost/low benefit: is it a necessary activity?

- High cost/high benefit: are current activity levels essential? Is it possible to develop methods at lower costs? Could output value be increased?

- Low cost/high benefit: this is your goal, so should activity be increased? Now, the opportunities can be identified.

The providers and users of the service should analyse, value and challenge the cost and benefits received and question:

- Can the activities be re-focused?

- Is there duplication or redundancy?

- What can be done to cut overheads?

- What would be the effect of eliminating the activity altogether?

- Can the activity be reduced in content, quality, frequency and quantity?

By this procedure, opportunities to improve the effectiveness of business methods will emerge, such as:

- Reduction of management layers.

- Simplification of reporting relationships.

- Focusing of responsibility and authority.

- Reduction of management complexity.

These rather pompous sounding proposals need to be reduced to a practical plan which shows: who does what, to whom and when. The results should be integrated into the business plan and budget and finally implemented.

Would-be entrepreneurs may well take the view that their business will not fall victim to bureaucracy. But, in my experience, every company – no matter how small – can benefit from a radical review of how well various activities serve their primary business objectives.

ADVICE

YOU AND YOUR ACCOUNTANT

What do you, the owner or manager of a small business, want from a professional accountant? I would venture to suggest that what you require may differ somewhat from what accountants *think* you require.

Accountants may believe that you want advice or literature regarding new areas of business, or indeed other businesses, while you may take the view that such matters are of little relevance to you or the problems you face.

In my experience, small businesses usually want their accountants to provide the basic services of audit, taxation and accountancy. Unfortunately, they do not rate important add-on services – such as business planning, project feasibility studies, tax planning, computer selection and advice on Europe – as priorities. What businessmen undoubtedly require is the efficient provision of basic services. This means that the partner, in the firm of accountants responsible for your affairs, must have:

- A comprehensive understanding of your business.
- A high-quality team.
- Personal skills and appropriate expertise.
- Independence and objectivity.
- A soundly based working relationship with you.
- Services that represent value for money.
- Continuity.
- Responsiveness to priorities and deadlines.

How does the start-up company decide which firm of accountants to appoint? There appears to be an inbuilt idea that small companies should use small firms of accountants because such firms are likely to be sympathetic to their objectives and will provide a more responsive and relevant service at less cost.

Major firms of accountants argue that this is no longer the case. They claim to provide a wider range of services and take the view that they are well equipped to take on small businesses and grow with them as requirements change. Most of the large accountancy firms have departments dedicated to providing services for small businesses under titles such as 'Business Services Group'.

The 'Big Six' accountancy firms perceive expanding small- and medium-sized enterprises (SMEs) as a key market and believe that their fees, while generally higher than those of smaller firms, represent value for money, particularly if their expertise is applied from start-up to flotation.

What are the key criteria which the business owner should consider when appointing professional accountants?

Initial thoughts may well focus on the firm's reputation, the expertise of the partner responsible and the fee scale. However, a more considered response should give priority to:

- Quality of work.

- Relationship between partner and client.

- Speed and efficiency of service.

The businessman may decide to receive proposals and/or interview two or three firms of accountants before reaching a decision. Such a procedure may be particularly appropriate in the case of a small business which has outgrown or become dissatisfied with its existing accountants.

Once an appointment has been made, the relationship between a company and its accountant is of paramount importance. The accountant must possess the personal skills to match the requirements of the owner or manager. These include a rapid response to requests, whether by letter, fax or telephone. There must be an element of 'he calls you' in the relationship, rather than 'you call him'.

The accountant should make a point of visiting you at your premises and, on his own initiative, should telephone you to ascertain how your business is faring and whether his advice might be of use.

Accountants should provide an efficient, speedy service and, most important, be available to speak to you and attend meetings.

The quality of work is, of course, an essential ingredient in the relationship, particularly as the appointment was probably made with this criterion in mind. Should the accountant's performance deteriorate, a loss of confidence is inevitable. This may well lead to a breakdown in the relationship and another accountancy firm being called in.

I can hardly conclude this subject without making some mention of fees. The first question often heard is: 'Aren't your fees rather high?' Fees are usually based on the time spent by the partner and various members of his team on a client's affairs. It should also be stressed that it is not general policy to offer discounts to new or small businesses. So the more pertinent question must be: 'Will I get value for money?' and then 'Can I get better value for money?'

PROFESSIONAL ADVISERS

It is imperative for owner-managers to recognise when they need professional advice and be prepared to take it.

Even small businesses require a wide range of professional advisers. These include:

- Chartered accountants: often a new business's first port of call, providing advice in respect of business plans, fund-raising and tax.

- Solicitors: advice on acquiring a business, preparation of agreements and patent rights.

- Chartered surveyors: advice on acquiring premises and how to obtain planning permission.

- Architects: advice on design and layout of premises.

- Insurance brokers: advice on insurance and the best way of obtaining it.

- Marketing consultants: advice on marketing, products and presentation.

All such advisers have one thing in common: they expect to be paid for their services. They may receive a fee, or may be remunerated on a commission basis, as is the insurance broker or the chartered surveyor who sells a property.

Professional advisers' charges are frequently criticised as excessive and unjustified. This is particularly so in the case of those who charge fees for their services, notably accountants and solicitors, but it should not prevent owner-managers obtaining advice when necessary. What is important is to ensure that the advice represents value for money. Only use advisers on relevant matters and for a specific period of time. Good advice is always worth paying for.

For small businesses, the choice is often whether to employ a large or small firm of advisers, particularly when it comes to chartered accountants and solicitors. The decision may depend on the business's size and aspirations.

Large professional firms can provide a wide range of services in a variety of locations, often on a worldwide basis. Such firms have a wealth of contacts and enjoy an international reputation which can rub off on a client: small businesses are sometimes judged by the company they keep.

Major firms produce numerous publications and also sponsor seminars which means that clients receive a considerable amount of free information and advice. Leading firms stress that they are well equipped to act for small businesses and argue that the range of services can develop as the business grows. To justify the use of a major firm, along with the higher fees, a client should be growth-oriented.

The advantage of using a smaller firm lies in personal service: the knowledge that someone is familiar with you and your business and will expend effort on your behalf. Although the range of services may be restricted it may be all that a small business needs. The firm's reputation will not be as great but this may not be important. Costs are crucial for a small business – particularly if it is to remain small – and in all probability their fees will be significantly less.

All of which brings us to medium-sized firms which, depending on your viewpoint, can be all things to all men or neither one thing nor the other. Fees may be less than those charged by large firms, particularly if such firms are situated outside inner-city areas. A personal service – often beyond the large firm – may be available. In the case of chartered accountants, many medium-sized firms have not been able to compete effectively and have merged with larger rivals. This trend is starting to apply to solicitors.

A businessman may choose to start with a small firm of advisers and graduate to a larger one. Then again, he may use two firms: one for general advice and another for specialist matters.

It will come as no surprise to hear that accountants and solicitors expect to be paid for their work. In the UK, it is not customary to spend a great deal of time on a project 'on spec' – on the basis that fees will be paid only if the project goes ahead, with minimal fees or nothing at all payable if it is aborted. All the same, there may be no charge for initial meetings, when the parties decide whether a project is viable and whether there is a basis for an ongoing relationship.

In order to restrict costs, a small business should decide what is required of its advisers, what it can carry out itself and what are the terms of reference for the adviser. Here are some suggestions for organising the early stages of a relationship:

- Work out and specify the services required of the adviser.

- Include these in the terms of reference or a letter of engagement to the adviser.

- Arrange to carry out any detailed or research work in-house, so far as it is within your capacity.

- Agree agendas for meetings with the advisers so that their involvement is limited to the matters which require their services. Remember: time costs money.

- Keep meetings as small as possible. It is not necessary to have teams of advisers all present at the same time.

- Agree the basis of charges in advance; then budget for the advisers' fees. Ask to be informed in advance if any overrun is expected and the reasons for it.

Once the relationship with advisers is established, make a plan for working together. It is important to have a point of contact in the advisers' organisation. In some cases, certainly with accountants, the relationship will be akin to a business partnership. It may be sensible to establish a regular pattern of meetings, with agendas, where concerns and plans can be discussed and advice obtained.

Business managers do not automatically follow the advice they are given. There should, however, be a good reason for not accepting such advice, otherwise it ceases to be value for money: the advisers will become frustrated and the relationship will prove unproductive. Another important aspect relates to advisers' fees; to get the best of service, payment arrangements should be adhered to.

There are occasions when advisers should be changed. You may become dissatisfied with their service and lose confidence. You may consider that you have outgrown the existing advisers. You may think the fees are too high and you do not receive value for money.

The first step should be to discuss the reasons for dissatisfaction with the existing adviser. If you still wish to change, careful consideration should be given before new advisers are appointed. There is likely to be a wide range of options. It may be the time to move to a large firm, particularly if the business is expanding. Before making such an appointment the usual practice is to ask a number of firms to submit written proposals and then hold interviews with two or three who appear to have the best credentials.

It is not difficult to find advisers in any field. Sometimes a firm or an individual expert is recommended by a friend or a business contact. An existing adviser, such as an accountant, solicitor or banker, may be able to suggest firms which will match a business's requirements. As a last resort, professional bodies usually have lists of names and offer a service which will recommend suitable firms. The Yellow Pages list all the names, should you really have to start from scratch.

It is important to organise professional advisers if you are to receive value for money. Many small businesses run up substantial fees for advice or services which are unnecessary. This is of little use to either party.

BANKS

CUMMINGS

LEARN TO LOVE YOUR BANK MANAGER

During these troubled times a forest of letters written by bank managers to their small-business clients will be consigned to the bin.

As far as some entrepreneurs are concerned, a deteriorating business and a mounting overdraft are marks of failure. Something embarrassing has occurred which they do not want to discuss and wish would go away. They do not want to take advice; they do not want to know.

Their hope is that if they do not communicate with their bank manager, accountant or colleagues, and do not open buff envelopes, the problems will disappear. They will not.

The bank manager is the man many businessmen love to hate. He is variously perceived as assassinator, torturer, headmaster or, at the least, spoilsport. The reality is that such fantasies are invariably conjured up by customers who have not found a bank suited to their type of business. Nor have they established a personal relationship with their bank manager a factor which inhibits regular communication.

The bank manager (like the accountant) should be familiar with your business and should visit you at your premises – on his initiative. He should be furnished with your annual accounts, business plan, management accounts and cash-flow forecasts.

Such information is essential, particularly if you have a borrowing requirement.

I am reminded of a discussion I had with Geoff Lane, Manager of Barclays Business Centre in Tottenham Court Road, regarding the current downturn in business. We touched on bank manager/client relationships and he stressed that what bankers are essentially looking for are long-term associations which are profitable to both parties and strong enough to withstand the occasional setback.

In his words: 'The bank does not expect to hear only good

news. A customer's problem may be the first opportunity for both parties to show their skills in adverse conditions. This can result in increased confidence and even stronger bonds for the future.'

It is hardly going to come as a complete surprise to your bank manager if, in the midst of the most severe recession since 1981, you show him management accounts and forecasts which indicate a downturn in sales and profits. If you keep the bank manager up to date with developments and progress it makes it easier to talk to him about additional facilities or a longer repayment period for an existing loan.

You must offer an explanation for your requests. There is little point in turning up for a meeting without a clear idea of the help you require. A vague, unprofessional approach will almost certainly result in a loss of confidence.

You should prepare a mini-business plan which includes revised profit and cash-flow forecasts. Any request for overdraft or loan facilities will be based on the revised cash-flow forecast.

If the bank provides special forms for such forecasts or if you have established a method of presentation which the manager is familiar with, stick to the procedure. Explain the variations from your earlier estimates and the assumptions made in arriving at your revised figures. Have at hand such evidence as is available to support your assumptions.

It is a good idea to involve your accountant in the forecasts: the bank manager will be that much more confident if he knows the figures have been reviewed by a professional.

It is important to make sure that the estimated maximum overdraft facility is adequate. While all is well if performance meets or exceeds forecasts, bank managers tend to lose patience with customers who habitually fail to meet forecasts and then return to ask for more.

Be prepared to answer questions in respect of the figures and your assumptions. It is often wise to have a colleague or an accountant with you who can add strength to your case.

You must also be prepared to negotiate not only the amount of bank assistance and the period for which it will be required but also the terms. Your bank manager will want to fix a rate of interest commensurate to the bank's risk, so reductions on this count are unlikely. He may, however, be prepared to work out a way in which the increased costs will not make a bad position worse – i.e. by charging exit fees or even taking an equity participation in the business.

Make your approach to the bank manager as soon as you realise you may need help. You will cause deep misgivings if negotiations are left to the last moment.

Provide a continuing flow of information to the bank manager. If you say you will provide information on a particular subject, make sure you fulfill your commitment.

Most bank managers want to be helpful but they must be conversant with the facts. As with so much in business, it is a matter of good communication.

BANKERS BEWARE

Many businessmen fail to achieve anything more than an arms-length relationship with their bankers. Clearing banks are the major providers of finance for small businesses but complaints abound. As 1992 approaches, the UK clearers face the prospect of competing with European, US and Japanese banks for small-business custom. Not least, the clearers will have to compete in terms of research into what services SMEs actually require, in contrast to the service they currently receive.

Bankers, for their part, are well aware of this potential threat and have duly responded. The 'Big Five' have gone to considerable lengths to attract small-business clients: note the recent spate of promotional activity in the shape of advertising and literature.

Such customers may be directed to business-centre branches which are specifically designed to offer services and advice for SMEs. All the same, owner/managers should bear in mind the fact that bank policies are centrally coordinated and cannot be tailored to meet individual requirements.

Although there is competition between the banks, this tends to centre around individual relationships between branch managers and customers, rather than a variety of options in respect of services and charges. Businessmen, depending on personal experience, may describe their bank as 'marvellous' or may use entirely different adjectives. In the event, either reaction reflects little more than the relationship between branch manager and client.

In my opinion, competition between the major UK clearing banks is largely superficial. Many businessmen take the cynical view that there is little point in changing banks because the services – and charges – are much the same.

The role of the banks is to provide a banking service, the key functions being to take deposits and make loans. The banks do not necessarily perceive themselves as risk-takers. This may come as something of a surprise to casual observers, given the clearers' record of lending to Third World countries and, at home, to overgeared corporations such as Bond Corporation, British & Commonwealth and Polly Peck. The textbook tells us that security and the ability of the customer to repay should be the primary considerations.

Against this background, the banks have widened their range of services which include advice and assistance in respect of:

- Business start-ups.
- Financial control.
- Book-keeping.
- Payroll operations.
- Pensions.
- Foreign payments.
- Direct debit.
- Credit-card facilities.

Banks, like all businesses, want to increase profits and a wider range of services is, in theory, one way of achieving this. Extra services invariably involve extra charges. It will come as little surprise to learn that the main areas of complaint concerning clearing banks are:

- Charges.
- Rates of interest for loans and overdrafts.
- Requirements for collateral security.
- Credit availability.

What SME customers want is not so much a wider range of services – many of which may not be relevant – but an improvement in the quality of basic services. The basic services which businessmen require are:

- Knowledge of their business.

- One-to-one relationships.

- Continuity of bank managers.

- Speed in decision-making.

- Accurate bank statements.

- Business advice.

These findings are borne out by a recent survey carried out by the Forum of Private Business and are similar to those obtained when SMEs were asked what they required from their accountants. The Forum's study indicates that the banks provide a higher standard of service than required in certain respects, namely: the breadth of services, access to bank loan officers and location.

But, in several key areas, there was a wide divergence between customers' expectations and the clearers' performance. This proved particularly so in terms of business and industrial knowledge, business advice and cheap loans.

The banks are aware of these findings and Alan Vaughan, marketing director of Barclays Bank's business sector, believes that the priorities of larger businesses fall into three main categories:

People: The quality of a customer's principal contact at a bank and the continuity of that contact and the quality of support staff.

Expertise: The bank's understanding of the business and its requirements.

Quality of service: Speed in terms of decision-making and the undertaking of instructions.

The reality is, however, that the banks could do more to foster closer relationships with the small-business community. This could be achieved by managers who research the affairs of their clients, keep abreast of relevant developments and meet owners/directors regularly – preferably at their premises.

A close and continuous relationship between the bank manager and client tends to ensure that areas of potential friction, such as bank charges and interest rates, can be dealt with before problems arise.

If a close relationship develops, the bank manager will automatically assume the role of business adviser – advice cannot be effective unless the giver and receiver are willing parties.

Meanwhile, the perception persists that banks are intent on providing the services they believe SMEs require. As I have already stressed, the priority on the part of the clearers must be to offer SMEs what they want. And if the Big Five do not deliver, then the French, German and Italian banks just might.

GOVERNMENT HELP

THE NETWORK

A decade ago, I and many others argued that small businesses had a major role to play in the revitalisation of Britain. Small businesses would create wealth, employment and innovation. Small business became a major initiative, flavour of the era for Margaret Thatcher's newly elected Conservative Government. Statistics showed that there were 1.25 million small businesses which employed six million people: one-quarter of our total workforce. They had mushroomed in all areas of industry, trade and the professions.

A series of Government measures designed to help small business followed:

- The removal of burdens imposed by planning and employment regulations.

- Tax incentives to encourage businesses to start-up and expand.

- Enterprise packages were introduced in three successive Budgets.

- Financial assistance in the form of grants and the Loan Guarantee Scheme.

At one time the number of measures taken to encourage small businesses totalled more than 100.

Small businesses flourished: their numbers rose and, after an interval, statistics confirmed that the small-business sector provided many of the new jobs that brought about an eventual decline in unemployment. In fact, employment became such a key issue that the Small Firms Minister and his department were transferred from Trade and Industry to the Department of Employment.

Is Government enthusiasm and support for small business still as strong? Witness the high level of interest rates?

Witness the introduction of the much-criticised Uniform Business Rate?

Support is still forthcoming but perhaps not in such direct and obvious ways. Now the emphasis is on creating an environment in which, as the language of 1992 would have it, SMEs can flourish. In the European Community, the talk is of small and medium-sized enterprises: no longer 'small businesses', considered by some to be old hat and somewhat vague.

In recent years we have seen the development of Business in the Community (BITC), which led to the opening of more than 300 Local Enterprise Agencies (LEAs): the first port of call for many start-up and embryo businesses.

Numerous new science parks, aimed at encouraging small, high-tech businesses, have been developed. The latest Government initiative comes in the shape of Training and Enterprise Councils (TECs) which offer services and advice in respect of a wide range of business and management skills.

A network is emerging between the various business advice organisations: the Training Agency is now joining forces with TECs, and the Business Growth training programme. They, in turn, are developing links with: the Small Firms Service, the Enterprise Initiative programme, the Youth Enterprise Centres, Inner City Task Forces, Local Chambers of Commerce and others.

The common theme is not to provide grants, soft options and easy money, although grants are still available under certain circumstances (in areas of unemployment and social deprivation). The policy is to make available advice and training in order to assist with business planning, accounting, marketing and quality control; the hope is that Britain's small businesses will modernise, innovate, become more efficient and so be better equipped to compete.

The burden of providing such services and creating an enterprise environment rests not only with the Government. By involving BITC, TECs and LEAs, the cost is passed on to the private sector: in reality, big business. It is the major companies which pay subscriptions and provide the secondees, goods and services which enable such organisations to function.

When I spoke to former Small Firms Minister, Tim Eggar, early in 1990, he agreed that the public perception of small business is relatively low key. This, he pointed out, in part reflects original success. Much was done in the 1980s to create a wide range of support measures and Eggar likened his position to that of a head waiter who is able to take customers through a comprehensive table d'hôte menu. Eggar's menu, courtesy of the Department of Employment, was a booklet entitled *Small Firms in Britain*.

Eggar stressed that Government policy had progressed from encouraging entrepreneurs to start up to second-stage support for the businesses founded in the 1980s which need to expand in the 1990s.

His hope was that small firms would increasingly use the services available from LEAs, Chambers of Commerce and TECs in terms of training, marketing and information technology. Equally, he hoped that such advice would, in part, be provided by experts from other organisations and businesses who might be prepared to spare some time (gratis) in view of the potential benefit to the community.

Eggar's perspective was that substantial Government funding was not required. In his eyes, the crucial factor was to establish a network and ensure that SMEs made use of the facilities.

Eric Forth succeeded Tim Eggar as Small Firms Minister in the summer reshuffle of 1990. One of his first initiatives was to commission a survey of owner-managed businesses. He followed this up by calling a conference to discuss the key issues and problems which had been identified.

One of the findings was that owner-managers do not make much use of the Government's services, with the exception of the DTI's Enterprise Initiative.

Forth wants to support the framework of assistance and measures currently in place and ensure they are used. He points to the 82 TECs which are assuming responsibility for many of the small firms schemes – with training usually a priority – which form part of the network linking with BITC, LEAs, the Small Firms Service, Youth Enterprise Centres, Inner City Task Forces, Local Chambers of Commerce and others.

The danger may be that too many sources of advice are available. Forth wants to do away with the concept of a host of separate organisations which all declare 'We are from the Government. We are here to help you.'

Forth's emphasis is to ensure that small businesses are an integral part of Britain's – and Europe's – business community and that their objectives, problems and achievements are recognised.

At the start of the 1980s, the Government's policies in respect of small businesses lagged behind many EC countries. Much ground has been made up but the majority of businessmen believe that new initiatives are still needed.

THE LOAN GUARANTEE SCHEME

After the Conservative Government came to power in 1979, it embarked on a programme of measures to help small businesses start up and expand.

One of the most innovative measures was the Loan Guarantee Scheme (LGS), which was introduced in 1981 and has proved the subject of only minor amendments. In the space of a decade, loans have totalled more than £880 million to some 27,500 concerns. Loans are currently running at the rate of 300 per month: well up to the Department of Employment's target.

The LGS encourages banks to lend to new or existing sole traders, partnerships and companies by guaranteeing 70 per cent of the loan (85 per cent in Inner Cities Task Force areas). Loans are for a maximum of £100,000, repayable over two to seven years, with the possibility of deferring the first repayment of principle for two years. In January 1988, a simplified procedure called small loan arrangements – in respect of loans of up to £15,000 – was introduced.

Loans must be for new or additional projects, not simply a conversion of existing loans or overdrafts. They are only available where normal bank lending is not an option – usually when no security can be offered or the business has no track record.

The scheme is open to small businesses with limited turnover or a limited number of employees. Eligible businesses include: manufacturers, retailers and most services. It is not intended for speculative ventures, such as property development or financial services.

Naturally there is a charge: currently 2.5 per cent of the amount guaranteed. This means that the cost to the customer should be 1.75 per cent of the total loan plus interest: in present conditions perhaps 17 or 18 per cent. In practice, banks may well charge the same rate of interest as on similar non-LGS borrowings, on the basis that LGS loans are more easily realisable and less risky.

Over the years, Government views on the scheme have sometimes been at variance with those of the lending banks. There were suggestions that the banks replaced high-risk lending with the LGS, along with criticism that some loans were not properly assessed − a factor which resulted in larger than expected losses, of which the Government bore 70 per cent (80 per cent during the scheme's early years).

There were also complaints that in certain instances the banks did not use LGS because of the administrative burden, or because bank managers were not sufficiently well versed.

Sometimes banks took the view that viable small businesses would be able to obtain loans through one of their own business start-up or expansion schemes. As for lending without security, it was all very well having the Government guarantee 70 per cent, but the banks were still exposed to 30 per cent.

Encouraged by the scale of demand, the Department of Employment's perspective is that 'the increase in popularity of the scheme since its relaunch, despite little publicity, indicates that there is a real underlying need for LGS funding.' Higher interest rates do not appear to have diminished demand or resulted in increased failure rates, which at 30 September 1990 were running at 30 per cent.

Bank statistics confirm the upward trend in the number and amount of loans. The total number of guarantees issued in 1988 was 1985 with a value of £55.58 million. In 1989 this rose to 3053 − value £96.72 million. By 1990 the respective figures were 3687 and £98.54 million. The aggregate from June 1981 to February 1991 is 27,988 guarantees: value £891.33 million.

Bank managers must, under the terms of the scheme, first consider conventional finance. Richard Cracknell, small-business manager at Barclays, and Stuart White, enterprise sales manager at Midland, agree that some managers are still reluctant to use LGS because they are unfamiliar with the details.

White, who was active in promoting small-loan arrangements, stresses that paper work has been minimised. In his words: 'We are doing all we can to educate our colleagues.' Andrew Hunter, NatWest's small business services' development manager, regards LGS as 'a useful product in the bank's portfolio, either as a stand-alone facility or part of a package'.

Geoff Lane, manager of Barclays' Tottenham Court Road Business Centre – a 'sharp-end' user of LGS – says: 'Over recent years I think the banks have tried to understand risk a great deal better and have been prepared to agree loans and overdrafts well outside the traditional lending criteria. In buoyant conditions things tend to go well, but in today's climate we may regret that we did not hedge some of our risk through schemes such as this.

'Some of the reluctance to use the LGS is based upon poor experience, for which we are partly to blame in forgetting that the quality of management is the first – and often the most difficult – issue to be tackled.'

The fact is that an LGS loan is one of the few sources of finance available to a new business where the proprietor has no security to offer. Friends and family may help and he can always approach the Local Enterprise Agency, but a bank loan is likely to be the best bet.

The value of the scheme is that it may enable a business to get off the ground, or expand, where it might otherwise have failed.

Another idea to improve the quality of lending and reduce bad debts is that applications should be accompanied by a business plan prepared with the help of a firm of chartered accountants. The accountants should then monitor progress. Fees would be added to the amount of the loan.

It has also been suggested that applicants should be required to have received some formal training in business skills.

As the calls on the Government's guarantee decline, it may be possible to reduce the premium from the current 2.5 per cent.

Some would like to see stricter adherence to the requirement that all personal assets – including the family home – should be pledged on conventional secured loans before an LGS is granted. Others take the view that the security requirements are too harsh and that enforcement would lead to a fall-off in the use of the scheme.

Many countries enjoy more generous schemes, with longer repayment periods and subsidised interest rates. My impression is that the UK scheme is about right: it balances the interests of businesses and entrepreneurs against those of the banks and Government.

BEAUTY OF THE BES

The Government's introduction of the Business Start-Up Scheme in 1981 proved a major innovation in terms of the provision of incentives for business investment in the UK. For the first time it became possible to obtain immediate income-tax relief on funds invested in new, privately owned companies.

In 1983 the scheme was renamed the Business Expansion Scheme (BES) and its scope was considerably widened; in particular, new investment in existing companies was included.

What is this scheme? How has it worked in practice? Can it be rated a success? The legislation is complicated, and what follows is a brief summary of the more important features:

- The BES is open to any UK resident.

- Income-tax relief is given at the individual's highest rate of income tax – currently a maximum of 40 per cent.

- The minimum investment which qualifies for tax relief is £500 in any one company, although BES fund managers usually require a higher minimum investment: often £2000.

- The total amount of relief given against an individual's income in any year of assessment cannot exceed £40,000.

- In the case of investments made between 6 April and 5 October, the investor can claim to have half of the relief related back to the previous tax year, subject to a maximum carry back of £5000.

- To qualify, the investment must be in the form of subscription for new Ordinary shares in an unquoted trading company. For this purpose an 'unquoted' company is one that is not quoted on the Stock Exchange or dealt in on the Unlisted Securities Market. Investment in an unincorporated business, such as a partnership, does not qualify.

• Relief is only given for genuine additional investment and may be withdrawn, in whole or in part, if the investor withdraws his funds from the company, sells his shares within the five-year period or breaks any other condition of the scheme.

• The BES covers most companies trading, wholly or mainly, in the UK, including those engaged in manufacturing, services, construction, retail and wholesale distribution. Investments which are excluded relate, in the main, to financial services and enterprises dealing in shares or land.

• The BES is intended for outside minority investors and not for proprietors who wish to invest funds in their own business. Relief will not be given where the individual (along with his associates) owns more than 30 per cent of the company's equity, or its assets, on a winding up. An associate for this purpose includes the investor's forbears, husband/wife or child but not brother/sister or other relative. Business partners and the trustees of certain family settlements are also 'associates'.

• Neither the investor nor any associate can be an employee or paid director of the company. This restriction is seen as deterring the owner-manager from investing in his own business and has been the subject of numerous submissions to the Chancellor of the Exchequer. However, the director or employee can be reimbursed for travelling and other expenses and he may receive fees for supplying services or goods on a normal commercial basis. He may also receive dividends on his shareholding.

Most conventional trading companies qualify for BES treatment. Exceptions include companies which deal in commodities, shares and land or provide financial, leasing, legal or accounting services. Special rules apply to businesses in wholesale and retail distribution to ensure that investments relate to bona-fide trading activities rather than to investment in assets, as might be the case with, for example, antique dealers and wine merchants.

Would-be entrepreneurs face an uphill task when it comes to setting up businesses from scratch; not least when the amount of capital is small: perhaps between £50,000 and £100,000. This is why businessmen usually take substantial financial risks at the time of start-up. Such risks often include personal guarantees along with significant loan interest and repayment commitments.

Banks are chiefly interested in providing loan capital and are reluctant to back new ventures – or provide additional capital for relatively new companies where rapid growth outstrips liquid resources – without a significant equity commitment on the part of the business owner.

In the event, it is often easier for small companies to seek finance from private sources. The Government's Loan Guarantee Scheme provides a useful facility for businesses which need to borrow up to £100,000.

The BES was designed to help fill the equity-financing gap by encouraging wealthy individuals naturally deterred by the high-risk element inherent in backing new or developing businesses to invest in unquoted companies.

With the cost of shares deductable for income-tax purposes under the BES, the eventual risk/reward ratio becomes that much more favourable.

MAKE THE BEST OF BES

I have attempted to explain how the Business Expansion Scheme (BES) is intended to help small businesses raise equity capital and summarised the legislation. The law remains complicated and any individual or company contemplating any BES investment should take professional advice.

From the start, the Business Start-Up and Business Expansion Scheme have been unpopular with the Inland Revenue – a factor which resulted in the original legislation being overlaid with anti-avoidance provisions. Then came a series of amendments which have served to emphasise different aspects of the scheme in the space of a decade.

In 1986, attempts were made to exclude BES relief for companies which enjoyed a high-asset backing and low risk. This meant that those companies in which property interests represented more than 50 per cent of net assets ceased to qualify. In the same year, tax relief was extended to cover capital gains, in that the first sale of an asset which qualified for BES was exempt from capital gains tax.

In 1988, the legislation took an entirely different turn. A restriction of £500,000 was placed on the amount which a trading company could raise through the issue of shares which qualified for BES relief in any one year. But, as part of the Government's policy for promoting private sector involvement in the expansion of rented housing, the acquisition and provision of property under assured tenancies was added to the qualifying list. In any one year, such companies were permitted to raise up to £5 million.

This legislation reduced the number of trading companies seeking BES subscription because the costs of raising no more than £500,000 appeared excessively high in terms of the amounts raised, while the risks were perceived to be as great as ever.

On the other hand, the measures stimulated applications for property-based companies which specialised in assured tenancies, where as much as £5 million could qualify for BES, and where the investment was, in any case, underpinned by the asset value. As a result, large property-oriented share issues dominated the BES market between 1988 and 1990. Critics argued that the BES should never have become mixed up with the Government's housing problems. Meanwhile, the £5 million maximum was also extended to companies involved in shipping.

Each year, venture capitalists and others who fund small businesses have called for amendments to BES legislation. Pressure mounted for an increase in the £500,000 maximum issue of qualifying capital for trading companies in any one year and, last year, the then Chancellor John Major, agreed to raise the limit to £750,000.

Pressure persists for a reduction in the time which shares must be held to qualify for BES relief – from five years to nearer three. This, it is argued, would encourage older and retired people to make BES investments.

Most constant of all is the argument that directors should be permitted to receive remuneration from the companies in which they make BES investments; possibly limited to £5000, but sufficient to encourage the individual to involve himself in the company in which he invests.

A further step would be to allow relief to the owner-manager, who might be drawing substantial remuneration. This has been resisted because it would be contrary to the scheme's basic objective: namely to encourage third parties to make minority investments in businesses which they do not control.

Since the Business Start-Up and Business Expansion Schemes began, the top rate of income tax has been reduced from 60 per cent to 40 per cent: it follows, therefore, that the tax relief has declined in value and attraction. Hence the belief that the scheme needs to be revitalised in order to compensate for the reduction in tax relief.

In recent years, the greater part of the public's investment has been in property-based companies, either those which offer assured tenancies or those with hotel, restaurant, healthcare or retirement-home interests.

Many such BES share issues have been open to direct subscription from the public. Others have been offered through BES funds which enable investors to spread their interests.

In 1989/90, BES offers declined and can be expected to decline further, particularly in view of the plight of the property market.

Despite the increase in the BES's fund-raising ceiling to £750,000 – for companies (other than assured tenancies) – this is still perceived as an expensive way of raising capital. An offer-for-sale prospectus (or similar document) is required to provide investor protection and the cost of sponsors, solicitors, accountants and the like, invariably absorbs a significant proportion of the funds subscribed.

The original purpose of the BES was to encourage individuals to take minority stakes in other people's businesses: businesses in the locality, businesses owned and run by friends or businesses which provide goods or services with which the potential investor is familiar and could make a positive contribution.

Perhaps the time has come to remove property companies from the list of businesses which qualify for BES relief. A welcome development would be the attraction of local BES funds into local companies, perhaps through the Local Enterprise Agency. In this manner, people's expertise and experience could prove of real value to the local community.

And, against such a background, Government should consider whether the BES can be made easier for investors. The reality is that the Business Expansion Scheme is faltering and, with tax relief at 40 per cent – which has diminished the attraction for private investors – it is not serving the businesses for which it was intended. It is a good scheme which should be rescued.

NOTHING VENTURED

VENTURE CAPITAL

Something of a mystique persists about 'venture capital' and 'venture capitalists'.

It is quite possible that a successful small business may have benefited from venture capital at some stage: during start-up, after its initial establishment or perhaps later when the business, albeit not ready for public ownership, had grown too large for the original owners to fund.

You may be under the impression that venture capitalists are only prepared to make equity investments in a few select enterprises or are simply in the business of lending funds. But in reality their involvement and support goes much further. Venture capitalists are not looking to invest funds, make a quick profit and get out. They see themselves as entering into a medium/long-term relationship with the businesses they support: more in the nature of a partnership to which the venture capitalist brings the benefit of his expertise and connections (as well as his money).

So don't be surprised should venture-capitalist organisations prove eager to:

- Offer advice.
- Put a director on the board.
- Spend time organising the enterprise in which they have invested.

This is not to say that venture capitalists are not in business to make profits. They are, and they take considerable care in selecting the ventures they believe will prove successful. As the British Venture Capital Association, which sets standards for the industry, puts it: 'Venture capital companies don't just sit back and watch their money work – they work with it; they not only back the company, they join it.'

There are more than 150 sources of venture capital in the UK, of which 124 are members of the BVCA. Statistics show a substantial increase in venture-capital investment during the past decade – particularly in the latter half. Some £5 billion has been invested since 1984, with 1989 alone accounting for £1.65 billion. More than 1500 companies benefited from venture capital in 1989: an average investment of more than £1 million.

There is a growing trend towards investment in Europe. Close on 100 European companies accounted for approximately six per cent of funds invested in 1989. Not surprisingly, the US is a significant market with 156 companies attracting eight per cent of funds.

No serious discussion of the venture-capital industry can pass without mention of 3i which must be regarded as the founder and leader of the industry. During 1989, 3i invested in 707 companies (38 per cent) with a value of £406 million (29 per cent).

The 1980s heralded an enormous growth in venture capital and indications are that the trend will continue. It is estimated that some £6 billion is currently available for investment in enterprises whose management teams match up to requirements.

More than £1.4 billion was invested in 1302 UK companies in 1989, the breakdown of which appears in the table on pages 89–93. Variations in percentages between the columns reflect the fact that funds invested in the average start-up or early-stage business are small compared with relatively few buy-outs and buy-ins, where investment can run to tens of millions of pounds.

It will be seen that venture capital covers several stages of a company's development.

Start-up

This is finance provided to companies for use in product and services development and initial marketing. It includes companies in the process of being set up or those which have only been operating for a short time. Some venture capitalists are not prepared to support start-ups.

Early stage

This includes finance provided for companies which are established and require further funds to start commercial production and achieve sales.

Expansion

This embraces funds provided for the growth and expansion of small businesses which have progressed through the initial stages of development and are seeking to expand by increasing production or developing new markets/products. Many businesses start out using capital provided by the entrepreneur, friends, relatives, and bank loans. They then look to venture capitalists to fund the next stages of expansion prior to a possible flotation or sale.

Management buy-outs and buy-ins

MBOs and MBIs enlarged the venture-capital market during the 1980s. An MBO involves the purchase of a major shareholding in a company by existing managers. The managers usually contribute a relatively small part of the funding in exchange for a controlling stake. An MBI relates to the acquisition of management control of a company by an experienced outside team.

Both strategies are attractive to venture capitalists because of the dual appeal of a proven business along with a management which obviously expects to improve on past performance. MBIs may be regarded as higher risk because the new management will, to some extent, be going in blind. MBOs and MBIs often require large amounts of venture capital which offer economies of scale to the capital provider.

Even so, the venture capitalists expect a return which compensates them for the risk taken in investing in an unquoted company which may well be highly geared. A pre-tax return of 30–40 per cent is not unusual.

MBOs tend to arise when:

- An activity no longer fits into a large group.

- A parent company needs to raise cash.

- A subsidiary is making losses or insufficient profits.

On the other hand, the initiative may come from managers who realise that their company is underperforming, that they may be in danger of losing their jobs, and that an opportunity is available to become proprietors rather than employees.

MBIs usually occur when a company has reached maturity and the owners are prepared to hand over management control to a new team in the knowledge that the business will continue. At the same time, talented teams are invariably on the look-out for precisely such opportunities to buy into. The trick is to introduce and match one with the other – a service which can be provided by the venture capitalist and one in which 3i has proved particularly adroit.

Venture capital takes various forms. More often than not the company, its advisers and the venture capitalist will agree a 'package' which will comprise part equity and part loan. The equity might be raised by a public offer of shares or a placing with financial institutions. Another possibility is for the investment to be made via a Business Expansion Scheme (BES) fund which, in turn, has raised money from the public; a pre-requisite being that the company must qualify for BES investment.

Equity can represent a combination of Ordinary and Preference shares and, where appropriate, Convertible or Redeemable Preference shares.

The funding package may also include borrowing on a medium/long term basis without causing further dilution of the equity. This can be facilitated by a straightforward term loan, with or without conversion rights.

Further refinements can ensure that the entitlement to equity, or the conversion rights attached to Preference shares or loan stock, are varied in relation to the company's success. In this way management can be given incentives or the venture capitalist can receive more protection.

NOTHING VENTURED, NOTHING GAINED

Within the small-business community, the general impression is that venture capital is difficult to obtain. Venture capitalists, for their part, argue that no worthwhile project goes unfunded.

But statistics show that only a small number of would-be entrepreneurs actually receive the venture finance required to start-up.

According to our research at Touche Ross, 60 out of 100 proposals are discarded after little more than a cursory glance and a further 25 after only a few hours study.

Although a considerable amount of time may be spent examining the remaining proposals, only five of the original 100 are likely to be regarded as suitable for investment. Even then, two of these will probably be dropped; all of which indicates odds of 33–1 against a venture-capital investment.

To narrow the odds, it is vital that your proposals are attractively presented. Once again, a well-prepared business plan is the key.

Venture capitalists regard a strong management team – with experience of the product/service and market – as essential. What they will look for is a balanced team which they would be happy to work with.

As with any investor, the venture capitalist looks for a distinctive product or service which will sell at the right price, and in sufficient quantities, to achieve a good return. It is important to demonstrate how the investment will be realised. Although the venture capitalist may be your partner, he will eventually want to reinvest his funds in another project.

The business plan should indicate what his investment might be worth at the end of a target period, and give details of how it might be realised: via a flotation, a sale to another company or a company buy-back of its shares.

It is important to approach the right venture-capital institution. In the UK, the majority are members of the British Venture Capital Association whose directory includes details of members, the amounts of capital available and the average size of investment.

In practice, the businessman seeking funds usually approaches a venture capitalist who is already known to him or one of his professional advisers.

Venture capitalists are not only interested in management teams; they will also take into account the quality of a company's advisers.

One oft-heard complaint — borne out by the table — is that venture capitalists are reluctant to invest funds of less than £50,000, £100,000 — or even £200,000.

In recent years, management buy-outs and buy-ins have proved a particularly profitable form of investment for venture capitalists. These usually involve substantial sums and appeal to venture-capital organisations because they are cost-effective and permit maximum effort to be channelled into a relatively small number of projects.

In view of the economic downturn, MBO and MBI activity has declined, a factor which signals leaner times for venture capitalists.

In this climate, venture capitalists must focus on new areas, and small businesses should benefit. Far too many venture-capital companies refuse to invest less than £200,000 or £500,000. A little more enterprise is long overdue.

MEMBERS OF THE BRITISH VENTURE CAPITAL ASSOCIATION
– INVESTMENTS AND FUNDING

Name	Capital invest (£)	Min Equity (£1000)	Type of funding	Start-up	Specialisation
Abacus Dev. Cap	2.7m	100	E	Y	I/M/F&D/P
Aberdeen Fund Mgrs	14m	50	E/L	Y*	—
Abingworth	120m	250	E	Y	T
Advent	125m	250	E	Y	
Advent International	300m	500	E/L	N	—
Advent Management OPP	50m	500	E	N	—
AIB Venture Capital	75m	200	E E/L	Y*	—
Alan Patricof Assoc	115m	None	E	Y	—
Alta Berkley Assoc	$65m	100	E	Y	HTE
Barclays Develop	87.9m	150	—	N	—
Barclays Ven Cap Unit	20m	100	E	Y	—
Baring Bros Hamb&Quist	ECU 140m	None	E	Y	—
Baring Cap Invest	ECU 150m	ECU 1m	E	N	—
Barnes Thomson	9.5m	100	E/L	Y	T
Baronsmead	59m	100	E	N	—
B'ham Tech (Vent Cap)	2m	20	E/L	Y	T
British Tech Gp	23m	50	E	Y	—
Brown Shipley Dev Cap	24m	750	E	N	—
Camb Cap Mgment	7.5m	200	E E/L	N	—
Candover Investments	356m	5m	E/L	N	—
Capital Partners Inter	—	10	E L	Y	—
Capital Ventures	71m	None	E/L	Y	—
Castleforth Fund Mgrs	6m	250	E/L	Y	Med
Causeway Capital	105m	500	E/L	N	—

Name	Capital invest (£)	Min Equity (£1000)	Type of funding	Start-up	Specialisation
Centreway Dev Cap	7.4m	150	E	N	—
Charterhouse Dev Cap	400m	250	E E/L	N	—
Charterhouse Vent Fund	48.5m	300	E	Y	H T Env
Chartfield & Co	48m	None	E E/L	N	—
CIN Venture Managers	100m	250	E/L	Y	—
Citicorp Vent Cap	—	500	E L	N	—
Close Invest Mngment	55m	300	E L	N	—
Clydesdale Bank Equity	—	250	E L	N	—
County NatWest Vent	—	250	EM	Y	—
Creditanstalt Dev Cap	—	350	EML	Y	—
Dartington & Co Sec	4.5m	100	E/L	MBO MBI	—
DCC Ventures	150m	1m	E	Y*	—
Derbyshire Ent Board	3m	50	EL	Y	—
Development Cap Gp	130m	200	E E/L	Y	—
Doncaster Ent Agency	1.6m	10	EL	Y	—
Dunedin Ventures	40m	200	E E/L	Y	—
Eagle Star Invest Mgrs	100m	500	F	N	—
ECI Ventures	150m	500	E	N	—
Electra Innvotec	33.4m	300	E	Y	—
Electra Kingsway	900m	2m	EM	Y	—
Electra Leisure	9m	500	EM	Y	—
Eurocont (Advisers)	ECU 35m	ECU 500	E	N	—
Fleming Ventures	20m	250	E	N	E T
Foreign & Colonial Vent	85m	500	E	N	—

Name	Capital invest (£)	Min Equity (£1000)	Type of funding	Start-up	Specialisation
Gartmore Investment	56m	300	E L	N	—
Granville & Co	125m	500	E D	N	—
Gresham Trust	—	250	E	N	—
Grosvenor Vent Mgrs	60m	500	E L	N	—
Guin Mahon Dev Cap (GPI)	15m	250	E	N	—
Gyllenh'mar Int	100m	500	E M	N	MI
Hambros Adv Tech Trust	8.65m	50	E	Y	TE
Hambro European Vent	28m	250	E E/L	N	P Man Fin
Hill Samuel Dev Cap	20m	500	E L	N	—
Hodgson Martin	14m	100	E	Y	—
3i	2bn	None	F	Y	—
ICI Invest Manage	18m	750	E L	N	—
Indus Dev Bd for NI	10m	None	E L	Y	Man
Industrial Tech Sec	3.5m	150	BES	Y	T
Ivory & Sime Dev Cap	130m	350	L	N	—
JIMI Advisory Services	1.4m	1	E	Y	—
Kleinwort B Dev Cap	100m	600	E	Y	—
Korda & Co	5m	None	E L	Y	T
Lancashire Enter	5.5m	50	E L	Y	—
Larpent Newton & Co	11m	None	—	Y	—
Legal & General Vent	200m	500	E M	N	—
LICA Development Cap	25m	100	E L	Y	—
Lloyds Develop Cap	100m	300	E/L	N	—

Name	Capital invest (£)	Min Equity (£1000)	Type of funding	Start-up	Specialisation
London Wall					
Invest	65m	500	E D	Y	—
Lothian	4.5m	50	E L	Y	—
March					
Investment					
Fund	13m	100	E L	N	—
Mercury Asset					
Mgment	—	500	E M	N	—
Midland Montagu					
Vent	171m	750	E L	N	—
MIM Develop					
Cap	120m	250	E L	N	—
MTI Managers	9.1m	250	E	Y	T
Murray					
Johnstone	200m	200	E/L	N	—
Mynshul					
Ventures	1m	25	E L	Y	—
NatWest					
Growth Opt	21m	5–25	E L	Y	—
Newmarket					
Vent Cap	33.5m	250	E L	Y	—
North of					
England Vent	19m	200	E/L	Y	—
Northern Vent					
Mgrs	25m	25	Flexible	Y	—
Norwich U					
Vent Cap	33m	250	E E/L	Y*	—
Oakland Inv					
Mgmnt	11.1m	400	E L	N	—
Oxford					
Seedcorn Cap	1.5m	10	E	Y	T
Phildrew					
Ventures	140m	500	E	N	—
Pine Street					
Investments	25m	250	E L	N	Fin
Piper Invest					
Mgment	7m	100	E	Y	RL
Prelude Tech					
Invest	14m	20	E	Y	T
Prudential					
Mgrs	250m	500	E	Y	—
Quayle Munro	20m	200	E L	Y	—
Rothschild					
AsseMgment	147m	$500	E	Y	T Med

Name	Capital invest (£)	Min Equity (£1000)	Type of funding	Start-up	Specialisation
Rothschild Ventures	44m	200	E	N	—
Schroder Ventures	450m	500	All	Y	—
Scimitar Develop Cap	$42m	300	E	N	—
Scottish Dev Agency	71m	50	E L	Y	—
Sec Pac Hoare Govett Eq Vent	—	500	E M	N	—
Sec Pac Vent Cap	300m	None	E	Y	—
Seed Capital	0.9m	5	E	N	T
Sumit Equity Ventures	55m	500	E L	N	T
Sun Life Inv Mgment	37m	250	Flexible	N	—
St James's Vent Cap	9m	250	E L	Y	T
Thompson Clive	70m	None	E	Y	—
Transatlantic Cap	8.5m	25	E L	N	Bio
Ulster Develop Cap	3.7m	50	E	N	—
Venture Founders	12m	100	E	Y	—
Venture Link Investors	21m	200	E	Y	—
W Midlands Enter Bd	19.5m	100	—	Y*	Man
Yorkshire Enterprises	31m	50	E L	Y	—

SPECIALISATION: Bio Biochemical; C Computers; D Distribution;
E Electronics; En Energy; Ent Entertainment; En Environment;
Eur Europe; Fas Fashion; Fin Financial; F&D Food & Drink;
H Health Care; I Industry L Leisure/Travel; M Management;
Man Manufacturing; Med Media; Medic Medical; MI Mature Industry;
O Overseas; P Property; R Retail; SB Service Businesses;
T Technology & Science; V Various.
TYPE OF FUNDING: E Equity; L Loan; M Mezzanine.

GOING PUBLIC

In the eyes of many small business owners, flotation on the Stock Exchange or entry to the Unlisted Securities Market represents the pinnacle of achievement. But the reality is that relatively few companies achieve a listing.

Some small businesses fail; others achieve a certain level of success and, having reached a sort of equilibrium, develop little further. Then again, many are sold or taken over, while others cease to exist in their original form.

High interest rates mean that many small firms currently find it difficult to maintain turnover and profits, so this is hardly a propitious time to contemplate USM entry, let alone a full Stock Exchange quote.

But, for the aspiring entrepreneur, it is never too early to plan for a flotation.

The advantages of going public are as follows:

- Existing shareholders can realise equity capital from the business.

- Further capital can be raised.

- Other businesses can be acquired by offering company shares.

- Admission to the stock market indicates that the business has been fully investigated which serves to enhance the status and credibility of the company.

But there are disadvantages:

- A public company comes under the scrutiny of a larger and more perceptive investment community.

- There will be a public expectation of growth and a greater degree of accountability on the part of directors.

- Significant costs are involved in flotation, many of which are ongoing in order to comply with Stock Exchange requirements.

- A public quotation might attract an unwanted takeover bid.

The most important source of equity capital is the general public – directly or through institutional investors – and the best way of attracting such funds is through the Stock Exchange.

There are many criteria for deciding how and when to float a company but, if the aim is a full Stock Exchange quote, the rule of thumb is that annual pre-tax profits should be not less than £1 million.

The USM provides a public market, with reduced compliance costs, for shares in small and medium-sized companies. A USM quote offers most of the advantages of a Stock Exchange listing, but only 10 per cent of the company's equity capital needs be released compared with 25 per cent in respect of a full quotation.

Companies which are unsuitable for full listings, because their trading record is too short, may be given permission to deal on the USM.

Under Stock Exchange rules a company entering the USM is obliged to make adequate disclosure of its affairs to ensure that an informed market is maintained in its shares, but the requirements are not as onerous as for a full quote.

Start-ups are occasionally floated on the USM, but the great majority are companies with established profit records. To all intents and purposes, pre-tax profits of companies seeking a USM float should not be far short of £750,000.

After an initial period of popularity USM floats have declined in number. MBOs and MBIs have been the trend in the last five years. For those companies determined to go public, it has usually been a case of a full quotation with USM a poor second alternative.

Significant costs, including fees for accountants, solicitors and sponsors, are inevitable and will vary depending on whether the entry is by way of an introduction, a placing or an offer for sale.

A placing or an offer for sale – taking into account requirements for a prospectus and an accountants' long form report – will cost something in the region of £200,000.

A public flotation is a major project and proprietors would be well advised to plan some three years ahead to ensure that the company is in the best possible shape when it comes to market.

The objective must be to present a sound profit record and balance sheet, along with prospects of further growth to attract investors.

As you draw up your flotation plan and timetable you should have the following matters in mind:

Advisers

You need to be supported by a team which will include a sponsor, stockbroker, reporting accountant and solicitor. These should be respected firms, active in flotation work and familiar with the company's type of business. You (and your company) may be judged by the company you keep, so choose advisors of good repute and make sure that the personalities work well together.

Sponsors

You need to appoint a financial institution, usually a merchant bank, to fill this important role. If you do not already have a merchant bank in mind your accountant will offer guidance. The job of the sponsor is to co-ordinate and drive the project forward.

Timetable

It is essential to have a timetable for the final months during the run-up to a float – and to adhere to it. The company's directors and senior staff will be fully occupied in providing information and attending meetings. They will have to delegate and there must be sufficient back-up support to ensure that the business does not suffer.

Method of entry

You and your advisers have to consider whether your Stock Exchange flotation, or entry into the USM, should be by way of an introduction, a placing or an offer for sale.

If your shares are widely held by the public (10 per cent for USM; 25 per cent for full quote) an introduction may be the most appropriate.

A placing may be appropriate for entry to the USM but, if the company is larger, then the limit on the amount which can be raised by a placing may well require an offer for sale.

An offer for sale requires more work and the costs, including such items as underwriting and advertising, are higher.

Management team

A potential investor will want to be satisfied that your company is well managed: at board level and below. It is important to ensure succession, perhaps by offering key directors and managers service agreements and share options. It is wise to draw on the experience of well-qualified, non-executive directors.

Capital structure

Any unattractive features, such as Preference shares with excessive dividend rates or shares or loan stock with unrealistic conversion rights, should be eliminated or adjusted before flotation.

The objective

The objective is to have a profit record which is rising but, in achieving this, you need to take into account directors' remuneration, pension contributions and the elimination of any expenditure which might be acceptable in a private enterprise but not in a public company. Excessive perks may take the shape of yachts, luxury cars, lavish expense accounts and holiday homes.

Accounts must be consolidated and audited to appropriate accounting standards and the audit reports must not contain any major qualifications. The auditors need to be satisfied that there are proper stock records and a consistent basis of valuing stock during the year prior to flotation. Accounts for the past three years (two years in respect of the USM) must be disclosed with the date of the last accounts within six months (nine months for the USM) of the issue.

Tax planning

This is a separate subject and proprietors should take advice to ensure that the shares are held in a manner which enables them to maintain control but also takes account of any long term intentions to transfer interests to other family members – a factor which may involve the creation of settlements, possibly overseas.

This could be the time to set up share option schemes for directors and employees. This may involve more than one class of share so votes are not necessarily pro rata to the value of the shares and dividend entitlement.

Reporting accountant

Once a company meets the basic requirements for going public, the reporting accountant becomes involved. A company's auditor may take on the reporting accountant's role, but if your auditor does not possess detailed knowledge of flotation procedures and Stock Exchange requirements it would be wise to employ one of the major firms to report, either jointly or on its own.

The reporting accountant will usually be asked to prepare a long form report: a detailed and confidential review of all aspects of the company's business which will be used as a basis for drafting much of the prospectus as well as a source of assurance to the sponsor and underwriter.

Such a report should bring to light any matters that require attention long before the issue and, similarly, should highlight significant strengths which will contribute to the issue's success.

Eventually, the reporting accountant will prepare a short form report to appear in the prospectus which will contain a summary of accounts and financial information for the previous three years.

The reporting accountant studies the company's business organisation in order to inform the sponsor as to the directors' ability to control costs and meet the profit plan.

Planning is crucial. You do not want to discover some 'showstopper' – such as an audit qualification – which effectively scuppers flotation plans.

If you are intent on going public do not be discouraged by the fact that profits are not yet high enough. Discuss your ambitions with your advisers. Go for it.

MANAGEMENT

TEAM WORK AND SUCCESSION

Most people, at an early age, ask themselves what they want out of life. What they put into life is another matter. By the time they reach their early twenties such thoughts may well become interwoven with work and business. 'Am I going to work for myself? Or for others?' Or conceivably: 'Am I going to work at all?'

Such questions should be repeated from time to time, not least by entrepreneurs.

Owner-managers gradually learn to appreciate the distinction between team-building in respect of business management and long-term planning for business succession.

Team-building should ensure that as a business expands and develops, it is managed by complementary and diverse staff in key positions.

Initially, there may be gaps. The entrepreneur may start-up on a solo basis but a team becomes essential by the second stage of development.

Banks, venture capitalists and outside investors will want to be satisfied that the business is managed by a suitably qualified team if funds are to be made available.

Individual roles, along with the relevant skills required, vary according to the business. In addition to a chief executive or managing director, other executive roles may include:

- Finance.

- Production and buying.

- Sales and marketing.

- Research and development.

- Personnel.

As the business develops, so the management structure changes. Different products may require specific skills, experience, and a presence in diverse locations – possibly overseas – which may lead to the appointment of additional directors or managers.

The Institute of Directors' survey, *Professional Development of and for the Board*, stresses the importance of team work, particularly among directors.

While this may sound all very well in theory, in practice, team building is difficult. Entrepreneurs experience special problems. Why should the entrepreneur – who as owner-manager made all the decisions and dealt with the problems – become part of a team?

Whether this is more satisfying than working alone, is answerable only by the entrepreneur. Owner-managers tend to find it difficult to shake off the belief that it is their business, so that finance and staff are their responsibility.

An entrepreneur may perceive the logic of delegation and shared responsibility but may not be able to come to terms with this in practice.

John Argenti, author of *Corporate Collapse: Cause and Symptoms*, wrote: 'If you have three or more of the following you are in the process of going belly-up':

- One-man rule.

- A non-participating board.

- An unbalanced top team.

- A lack of management depth.

- A weak finance function.

- A combined chairman and chief executive role.

Professor David Storey of Warwick University promptly responded: 'Simply not true', but at a recent Owner-Manager Conference, some scored five out of six.

This demonstrates the owner-manager's natural inclination to do everything himself and bears out the Institute of Directors' finding that more than 90 per cent of directors had received no specific training in respect of their boardroom roles.

The owner-manager's prime responsibility is to direct the business. He must have time to think, develop strategies and be creative. To do this properly he must delegate detailed business operations; which requires a team qualified for such responsibilities.

Bob Garratt, chairman of the Association for Management Education and Development, who has lectured on team-building, has outlined certain areas where owner-managers are apt to get their priorities wrong.

They tend to:

- Go for action and growth rather than thought and profitability.

- Rely on telling people what to do rather than developing their skills.

- Fail to understand the difference between chairing, as opposed to leading meetings.

If the board consists of family or friends there may not be a diversity of perspective nor the inclination to develop and keep up to date. A business may develop symptoms of old age and gradually decline, with negative effects for owner-managers, employees and shareholders.

Garratt has suggested that owner-managers should set themselves a target date by which time they should have a strong team in place to deal with the detailed business operations within an agreed plan. Then the owner-manager can devote his time and skills to:

- Policy formulation and strategy implementation.

- Debating ideas before making judgments.

- Encouraging education.

- Provision of sufficient support and criticism to ensure the business's survival.

Not that succession is necessarily resolved by such methods. Owner-managers can be members, perhaps captains, of their team without any clear conception of purpose, in either personal or business terms.

His objectives may be:

- To sell out, withdraw substantial funds and retire.

- To sell a major stake but continue working, perhaps with further remuneration paid on an 'earn-out' basis.

- To keep the business operational so that his children can take active roles and possibly succeed him as owner-managers.

There are subsidiary questions:

- Will retirement lead to other occupations and activities?

- Should the owner-manager continue in the business? If so, for how long, and in what capacity?

- If the business is to be inherited by children or associates, do they possess the relevant skills, training and commitment?

- Will partners or colleagues agree with such a decision?

Once such questions have been taken into account, professional advice should be sought in respect of capital-gains and inheritance-tax consequences. It is essential that such transactions are timed to maximum advantage.

Above all, it is essential to ensure that the succession is in good hands — unless a sale is intended, in which case that is a problem for the future owners.

Succession may not mean promotion for an existing team member or the appointment of a newcomer to assume control. It means ensuring that the directors are able and committed to the continuation of what the owner-manager started.

Businesses do not stand still: they either progress or decline. Succession must be planned before the owner-manager burns himself out.

CASUAL EMPLOYMENT

The employment of casual labour is full of pitfalls and many employers, particularly small businesses, are not fully conversant with the relevant income tax, PAYE and national insurance regulations.

If employers do not comply with such regulations at the time of paying casual staff, they run the risk of having to pay any outstanding tax and national insurance contributions – plus substantial penalties – without being able to recover any such payments from the casual employees concerned. To this must be added the cost of investigating such discrepancies.

The relationship between employer and employee is effectively a 'contract of service' – written, oral or merely implied – which applies even if the employment is casual, part-time or temporary. A contract of service can be said to exist if the employer is entitled to require the presence and attention of the employee and to direct and control the manner in which the employee performs tasks entrusted to him.

The employee, for his part, can expect the employer to provide work and reward him at an agreed rate. When a contract of service exists, the provisions of the Employment Acts and the regulations covering PAYE, income tax, national insurance contributions, statutory sick pay and statutory maternity pay, apply.

It is the employer, irrespective of whether he recognises himself as such, who bears the responsibility for applying PAYE and national insurance regulations. If it is held that there is an employer/employee relationship, it is the employer who is responsible for such liabilities. An employer cannot shuffle such responsibility on to the employee unless he receives Inland Revenue authority to the effect that the individual is not subject to PAYE tax – such as the issue of a 'No Tax' coding.

It is not the case, as some employers appear to believe, that cash payments relieve them of such responsibilities. Tax rules can be summarised as follows:

- If the casual employee provides a P45 from a former employer, the normal PAYE procedures should be followed, irrespective of the length of employment.

- If the casual employee's contract is for one week or less, and a P45 is not produced, income tax, in accordance with the tax tables on a week-1 basis, emergency code, must be deducted if the gross pay is more than the weekly tax threshold: £63.50 for 1991/92. Details of the casual worker's name, address, NI number, gross pay and income tax deducted must be recorded on a Deductions Working Sheet to provide support for the information which will be included in the end-of-year tax returns to the Inland Revenue.

- If the casual employee's contract is for more than one week – or if an initial contract of one week or less is extended – and a P45 is not produced, a P46 should be prepared and the employee must sign either Certificate A or B on the front of the Form.

- If the total weekly pay is greater than the £63.50 weekly tax threshold, a Deductions Working Sheet must be prepared with the same particulars as before. If the employee signs Certificate A on the P46, tax should be calculated at the basic rate – 25 per cent for 1991/92. In each case, the completed P46 should be submitted to the Inspector of Taxes who administers the employer's PAYE scheme and Form P15 (coding claim) should be issued to the employee, details of which he should submit to the Inspector.

- If an employee is employed again within the same tax year and a P45 is still not produced, the procedures must be repeated and a separate Deductions Working Sheet prepared. Payments should not be aggregated with previous periods of employment, whether casual or permanent.

A P45 must be issued at the conclusion of the contract to each casual employee for whom a P45 or P46 has been submitted to the Inspector of Taxes, whether or not PAYE income tax has been deducted.

Details of casual employees, for whom a Deductions Working Sheet – which shows tax and/or NI contributions paid – has been prepared, should be included in the employer's annual statement Form P35 at the end of the tax year. If any casual employees have received more than £100 in the tax year – although no Deductions Working Sheet was prepared because individual payments were below the threshold – details of those employees, along with total payments made, must be submitted to the Inspector of Taxes on an Employers' Supplementary Return Form P38A.

National insurance is dealt with in a similar way, but the earning limits are lower than for income tax:

- NI contributions must be paid by the employer and the casual employee whenever weekly pay reaches the NI lower earnings limit – £52 for 1991/92 – regardless of the days worked in the week.

- Contributions must be recorded on the Deductions Working Sheet which was established for tax records. If a Sheet has not been created, because the total week's pay was less than the £63.50 tax threshold, it must be prepared and include: the name, address, NI number, gross pay and NI contributions – total and employee proportions.

If the weekly gross pay reaches the lower earnings limit of £52, but not the tax threshold, a note should be made on the Sheet to show that it has been created for NI contributions only. National insurance contributions are not due if the weekly pay is below the NI lower earnings limit.

The maximum amount, in a fiscal year to 5 April, which may be paid to a casual employee, which will not require the application of PAYE or NI procedures, is £100, of which no more than £51.99 (for 1991/92) may be paid in any one week. Even then, it is necessary to keep details of names and addresses and amounts paid.

It is the employer's legal obligation to comply with the regulations, even if the casual employee makes an income return each year.

While it may not be necessary to withold income tax or NI contributions at the time of payment, on the basis that they are lower than the thresholds laid down, the employee may be liable and is obliged to include all payments received in his personal tax return. The Inspector of Taxes may ask various employers for confirmation of the amounts paid, even in cases where they amount to less than £100 in the fiscal year.

Students enjoy special arrangements. If a student declares that his/her total statutory income for the current tax year will not exceed the single person's personal allowance for that year – £3295 for 1991/92 – he/she must complete Form P38(S).

No income tax is payable on a student's vacation earnings, but such earnings are still liable to NI contributions. A student's earnings in respect of weekend or evening work, other than during the vacation, are not subject to this special arrangement and should be treated in accordance with normal casual employment rules.

It is essential that the employer does not accept that a person is self-employed, merely because the employee informs him of such. The employee should be asked to provide the name of the income tax district which deals with his tax affairs, along with the reference.

The employer should then request the Inspector of Taxes dealing with his PAYE scheme to confirm the position and advise the coding to be operated by referring to the employee's Inspector. If the employer's Inspector is satisfied that the earnings will be dealt with on a self-employed basis, then a coding will be issued confirming that no tax should be withheld.

Failure to comply with the regulations carries penalties. This embraces failure to include casual worker's payments on Form P35 or Form P38A and failure to retain records sufficient to identify those who have received payments.

For national insurance, a sweep-up clause operates which imposes penalties for breach of or non-compliance with any regulation. Employers must familiarise themselves with *The Employers' Guide to Pay as You Earn* and *The Employers' Guide to National Insurance Contributions*.

You have been warned.

BUSINESS INSURANCE

'Get the strength of the insurance companies around you' read an advertisement that caught my eye: a message which is indeed valid for today's businesses. Small businesses should ensure that they have a competent insurance adviser – not just a salesman for a particular company but a broker who can review requirements and arrange a full range of insurance cover at competitive prices.

Using an insurance broker is no more expensive than dealing directly with an insurance company, and a broker should provide objective professional advice.

Insurance advice is not just a one-off exercise. The broker should review his client's insurance policies and the amount of cover on a regular basis. If the broker's service is unsatisfactory, others may be only too happy to offer preferable terms.

Insurance is not a one-way business. It is essential that insurers are notified of any change in circumstances which may affect a policy. It is not sufficient to contact insurers only when you want to make a claim.

It is always stressed that insurance is a contract of *uberrimae fidei* – utmost good faith. Inclusion of any incorrect information or failure to fully disclose all known facts, can make the insurance null and void.

Certain insurance is a legal requirement:

Employers' liability
This is a statutory requirement for employers. Such insurance covers employees against death or bodily injury sustained in the performance of their work. Premiums are usually calculated as a percentage of the payroll and cover is traditionally unlimited.

Motor vehicles third party
Third-party insurance cover on all motor vehicles used on

public highways is essential but comprehensive cover is generally recommended.

Specified equipment
Insurance and regular inspection, normally by insurers, is mandatory for certain equipment and machinery, such as lifts, boilers and pressure vessels.

Property or equipment under lease
A requirement for insurance cover is usually stipulated in a lease for rented premises. The leasehold obligations for buildings vary considerably for both structural damage and the implications of the rent cessor clause. Such complex conditions should be referred to the tenant's broker for advice.

Most contracts require insurance for leased or rented items – whether it is a piece of machinery or a computer system – as if it was the property of the lessee. Banks and other lending institutions usually insist that the assets on which a loan is secured are insured. In some cases life assurance is required as additional security.

When selecting insurance cover, it is necessary to consider the reasons for taking out insurance. Is it to seek reimbursement for expenditure which might be incurred as a result of loss or damage – claims which, although inconvenient, could be borne by the business? Or is the purpose to insure against disasters and occurences which could ruin the business? In my opinion the latter is the correct approach for a privately owned business.

Remember that insurance companies are in business to make money. Out of the premiums they receive, only some 60–70 per cent is usually paid out in claims. This does not mean that insurance should be disregarded altogether, but rather chosen selectively. Be prepared to pay a set amount of any loss or claim yourself.

With such thoughts in mind, the business owner should review the following areas of risk:

Premises
These must be insured against fire, lightning, explosion, aircraft and usually storm, flood and subsidence. In the case

of a full repairing lease, accidental damage should also be considered.

Plant, equipment, furniture
These will usually be insured against fire, water damage and in some cases theft and accidental damage.

Stock and work in progress
Similarly, these will be insured against damage or loss from fire, water, heating failure or whatever other risks may be applicable. In most cases insurance against theft is necessary.

Cash
Loss as a result of theft is usually covered under a cash in transit policy.

Fidelity insurance
This can be arranged to cover misappropriation by employees.

Motor vehicles
I have noted the legal requirement for third-party cover: many businesses will extend this to full comprehensive cover but perhaps with an excess, so that the first £250 of each claim, for example, is met by the business.

Loss of profits
In the event of a disaster, such as serious fire damage, a business may not be fully operational for some time. Most of the business costs, particularly salaries, continue, while the drop in income reduces or eliminates profit. Losses can also result from the destruction of accounting records or computer breakdown. Disruption may also arise if a major customer or supplier suffers a serious loss.

There is a range of insurance policies to protect employers, employees, customers and the general public:

Public liability
This may be part of the contents policy. It is necessary to insure against the possibility that a visitor to business premises, or a passer-by, is injured.

Product liability
This is as important as public liability. Such cover offers

protection against claims arising from accidental damage or injury involving a company's products.

For manufacturers, retailers and restaurateurs, there is a risk that a product may be faulty and cause injury or illness to others – toys and pharmaceutical products spring to mind. Insurance can assist in meeting such claims.

Permanent sickness and disability

While not essential, the business owner may choose to insure against the prolonged sickness of senior executives and staff. Such a policy provides a cushion if a key colleague departs and may prove an attractive element in a remuneration package, on the basis that the funds will be used to cover salary during illness.

Personal accident

Many businesses take out such insurance in order to provide a lump sum in the event of the accidental death or injury of a director or employee. This can be extended to provide cover for travel, injury abroad and loss of baggage. Insurance in respect of permanent sickness and personal accident are best arranged on a group basis: when the risk can be averaged, the premium is proportionally less.

Key-man insurance

Where an individual is key to the success of a business, the firm can be insured against his death or injury. Any insurance recovery helps compensate for any deterioration of business under such circumstances. Banks may require such cover if a business plan relies heavily on particular individuals.

In recent years it has become commonplace to sue suppliers, advisers and any other party involved, if goods or services are found to be faulty and damage has resulted. This has led to a range of policies designed to protect the business against negligence, or failure to observe legislation or a contract by directors, partners and employees.

Directors' liability

The Insolvency Act 1986 increased the likelihood of a company director being disqualified and made personally liable for company debts. Breach of duty, failure to keep proper records, file documents and call meetings, along with other failures to observe legislation, can be covered by a 'Directors' and Officers' Insurance Policy'.

Professional indemnity

No major professional firm would consider operating without professional indemnity insurance: the risks and claims could spell disaster. Some professional organisations require minimum limits of insurance cover for members. Such cover and the excess required is a matter of judgment.

Credit insurance

The Export Credits Guarantee Department offers a trade insurance service which is familiar to exporters. An exporter can insure with ECGD against the risk of not being paid for goods. It is also possible to obtain cover against the imposition of exchange controls, political risks and war.

Not so well known is the fact that credit insurance is also available for home markets. A most effective use of credit insurance is to protect against disaster: should bad debts exceed the amount a business can bear. Certain insurance brokers specialise in this area.

The key factors to remember are:

• Use a good insurance broker.

• Be prepared to compare the service you receive with alternative proposals.

• Do not take out unnecessary insurance.

• Review insurance cover regularly: if you are under-insured it may not be possible to recover the full amount of loss.

THE HIGH-TECH JUNGLE

Businessmen often point out that their priority is to look after the shop rather than keep books and fill in forms.

The outcome, as often as not, is that at the end of the financial year the books are in a state of disarray and time and money must be spent in order to produce accounts.

Organising books and records is a common problem for start-ups and small businesses, but it is essential that accounts are kept in order, before major problems develop such as cash-flow difficulties and inaccurate PAYE and VAT returns. Such problems can result in serious penalties.

Some business owners take the view that a computer is the answer to their problems, but this is not necessarily the case, particularly for small businesses where there are perfectly adequate manual systems. You do not need a computer to be efficient. Nor is a computer a status symbol.

Having said this, a successful business will eventually need to consider investing in a computer. Computers offer the entrepreneur a range of useful facilities:

- Accounts: monthly management accounts, including analysis of profit-and-loss account and balance-sheet items.

- Financial control: programmes for matching performance against budget and for monitoring cash flow, with the facility to update throughout the year.

- Processing orders, stock control and invoicing: a computer can improve and possibly replace manual proceedures in your office.

- Wages and PAYE: a computer will keep records, make calculations and provide information for Inland Revenue and Social Security purposes.

- Word processing: a computer can effectively replace

typewriters and speed up quotations and mail shots. The end-product, involving as many copies as you require, should be of a high standard.

- Database: a computer can store information on customers, contacts, stock and employees − factors which should cut down on research and filing time.

When selecting your first computer, you should:

- Seek professional advice to identify a suitable supplier. Scores of computers and hundreds of accounting packages are available.

- Decide on the computer and software required before you buy. Do not rely on the salesman of a particular computer or software company.

- Ensure that your business records are properly organised before you convert them to computer or you may end up in a worse situation than before.

- List your requirements and request detailed proposals, including installation plans, training methods, timetable and full costings from selected suppliers.

- Ask suppliers for their client lists and permission to request references from customers to ensure they are satisfied with the products and services provided.

- Before committing yourself, ask to see similar installations working and processing in another firm's office. You want a tested and effective − not experimental − system.

- Spend time selecting the correct system with the appropriate back-up support. Make sure that you do not choose something which is about to become obsolete. Do not make your choice solely on price.

- Ensure that you obtain a system which not only copes with your current transaction volume but can easily be expanded to meet future requirements.

- Do not allow yourself to be overwhelmed by computer

salesmen's jargon. Do not rush into a decision and do not hesitate to take independent advice.

- Ensure that your staff are trained to operate the system and, if necessary, enlist the supplier's assistance.

- Check the price carefully, particularly the quotations for maintenance. A computer can cost twice as much – and take twice as long to install – as salesmen claim.

The capacity and efficiency of micro-computers have improved enormously in recent years, with the result that they are extremely cost-effective for small businesses and sufficiently powerful to meet the needs of relatively large businesses. At the same time, the range of software has expanded and can provide solutions to numerous business problems. Software packages include:

- Order processing, invoicing and debtors ledgers, sales analysis, stock control, purchasing and creditors' ledgers and job-costing.

- Nominal ledger and management accounts.

- Payroll, time analysis.

- Cash-flow forecasting and budgeting.

- Word processing, direct-mailing facility, telex and fax dispatch.

Should you have difficulty finding a package which meets your requirements, programmes can be prepared specifically for your business. This, however, is expensive and time-consuming for small companies.

Technical advances in micro-computers enable small businesses to improve many aspects of operations. With an in-house computer you can:

- Respond more quickly to computer orders.

- Identify your best customers and analyse the products and services they buy.

- Keep records of the profitability of each product you sell.

- Implement cash collection from your debtors.

- Maintain stocks at minimum levels for efficiency in conjunction with a re-ordering system, which reduces the risk of running out of particular lines.

- Check the arrival of purchases and ensure that you take advantage of discounts available for prompt settlement.

- Predict low points in your cash flow so that you can arrange banking facilities in advance.

- Monitor the business efficiently in order to take prompt action should things go wrong.

- Present mailshots, reports and management accounts more professionally.

A computer can ensure that the small firm develops faster, cutting down on some of the time-consuming chores and avoiding mistakes which might otherwise occur. It can enable you to cope with increased business volume without necessarily adding to your overheads. But it is important not to buy a computer before you are ready for one and, when you are ready, to choose the system which is best suited for your particular business.

VAT: IT PAYS TO GET IT RIGHT

I would like to sound two warnings regarding VAT penalties.

The first is relevant to businessmen who are already registered for VAT. The second concerns those who are about to start a business or have recently started up but are not familiar with the requirements to register for VAT.

Following the Keith Committee report in 1983 the procedures for administrating VAT were tightened up. These include provisions for charging interest and penalties where inter alia returns are submitted late or where mistakes have occurred.

During 1989, after the decisions made by the European Court of Justice, legislation and regulations were introduced in the UK so that transactions in several categories where VAT was previously zero-rated are now charged at the standard rate of 17.5 per cent. These include sales of new non-domestic buildings and the construction and alteration of non-domestic buildings.

Such transactions are likely to involve substantial amounts which means that any penalties and interest charges, due to mistakes, could be significant.

Misdeclaration penalty

As from 1 April 1990, Customs and Excise (responsible for the administration of VAT) imposed a 30 per cent penalty in respect of serious misdeclarations of VAT. This was reduced to 20 per cent in the 1991 Budget while Customs and Excise carry out a survey of the penalty structure. The penalty is calculated in relation to the tax which has been lost and applies in any period when there is an error in the amount of tax declared which exceeds either 30 per cent of the true amount of tax due, or £10,000 or five per cent of the true amount of tax due – whichever is the greater.

It is unlikely that the first of these yardsticks will apply where the VAT owed is small: for example, where a £5000 declaration of VAT payable is subsequently amended to £7500. In contrast, a declaration of £500,000 amended to £540,000 results in an error of £40,000 which is greater than £27,000 (five per cent of £540,000).

However, the penalty can be avoided by disclosing any error of more than £1000 to Customs and Excise before it comes to their attention, either by letter or by using form VAT 652. If the error is less than £1000 it will be sufficient to make an appropriate entry in the current VAT return.

In any event, interest will be payable at a commercial rate on any under declaration from the date the return was due, whether or not a misdeclaration penalty is charged.

Such interest will not be allowable for income-tax or corporation-tax purposes.

Regulations have been introduced which, in addition to normal VAT accounting arrangements, will require a separate VAT account to be maintained for each VAT accounting period and for this to be corrected as errors come to light.

These regulations make it more important than ever to get your VAT accounting right first time.

Penalty for failing to register

When a person who should have registered fails to do so he is liable to a penalty based on the tax which would have been charged. A delay not exceeding nine months: 10 per cent; between nine and 18 months: 20 per cent; more than 18 months: 30 per cent.

In these circumstances, penalties are likely to prove severe. Not only will the trader have to pay more than the VAT he should have charged his customers – possibly going back over a period of months, plus the penalty – but he may find it difficult (if not impossible) to subsequently recover the VAT from customers.

A person, partnership or company is required to apply for registration for VAT if:

- At the end of any 12-month period taxable supplies exceeded £35,000 (previously £25,400).

- There are reasonable grounds for believing that the value of taxable supplies over the next 30 days will exceed £35,000.

In all cases these amounts exclude VAT.

These limits may be varied by statutory instruments but in practice they are normally charged in the Budget.

There are other VAT penalty provisions in operation for:

- Criminal offences − falsification of VAT returns or claims. This can carry an unlimited penalty and possible imprisonment.

- Civil fraud − dishonestly evading tax. This can involve a penalty up to the amount of tax evaded.

- Unauthorised issue of tax invoices. The penalty is 30 per cent of the tax incorrectly charged or £50, whichever is greater.

- Default surcharge − for repeated failure to submit returns within one month of the end of the VAT accounting period. The penalty starts at five per cent of the tax involved, rising to a maximum of 30 per cent for repeated offences.

- Breaches of VAT regulations − failure to keep records, supply information or notify cessation of trade.

- Persistent misdeclaration − material inaccuracies in any two returns within a two-year period.

Faced with a penalty a trader may offer a defence of 'reasonable excuse'. This is strictly interpreted and does not include: insufficient funds; relying on another person or delay or inaccuracy on that person's part; ignorance of the law; pressure of work; difficulty in forecasting annual turnover; or errors in calculations.

Nor does it include a claim that there was a notification to register but no evidence that it was pursued (Customs claim they record all registration inquiries).

VAT regulations are tough and the Customs' interpretations harsh. It pays therefore to take trouble over your VAT returns — tiresome as businessmen find them. Get it right first time.

CRISIS MANAGEMENT

A businessman recently telephoned me: his business was in difficulties; sales had fallen; his workforce was idle; the bank overdraft was going up; what should he do?

His problems are typical in today's climate. The question which all too many owner-managers are attempting to answer is: how do I make my business more profitable, or indeed, profitable at all?

There are only three ways to increase profits – or reduce losses. The first takes time to be effective; the second and third are more immediate:

Increase sales

Can you sell more of the same to new markets, in Europe for example? Or could you sell through mail order?

Could you develop and sell a new product or service to new or existing customers? Could you widen your range, change your style or develop a new product?

Is it possible to change your sales mix to include more items with high margins and less where margins are thin?

Price increase

This requires careful research. If you raise prices, will volume fall? By how much can you put prices up before the fall in volume reduces gross profit rather than increases it? Can you compensate for higher prices and lower volumes with new lines or new customers?

Can you compensate for lost volume through advertising and marketing?

Difficult questions to answer. Before making any decisions you should check customer reaction and take note of what the competition is doing. You should also research the opportunities for new markets and the demand for improved or new products.

Cutting costs

This is usually the first area for attention, one where results can be estimated with some accuracy and achieved quickly.

The first requirement is a strict system of cash control. Cash-flow forecasts should be prepared and monitored regularly. Always bear in mind the amount of sales turnover required to cover each £100 of overheads.

Next, review each expense heading to see where savings can be made. This review should fall into two parts: firstly, an examination to ascertain whether costs can be reduced by 'good housekeeping' and secondly, whether significant policy changes should be adopted. Such changes might include replacement of equipment, more efficient production procedures or a cut in advertising expenditure.

- Bank interest: can the overdraft be reduced by improved invoicing and cash-collection procedures? Could invoices be sent out earlier? Are invoices carefully checked in order to avoid errors which may lead to costly delays and disputes with clients? Are payment terms clearly stated? Is there a procedure under which late payments are pursued? Remember, a personal phone call is often the most effective way of ensuring payment. Are cheques paid in promptly? Your bank manager may be able to facilitate early clearance of cheques.

- Good housekeeping: can better terms be negotiated with your existing supplier? Or another supplier? Could an alternative supplier provide raw materials cheaper?

- Stocks: could you make do with lower stocks of materials and finished goods? Could you establish lower levels of stock before re-ordering? Could the stock-control system be improved to produce more up-to-date information regarding stock levels?

- Use of staff: could productivity be improved by re-organising work schedules or working conditions? Could the number of staff be reduced – perhaps by natural wastage? Is the staff mix correct – could you do better with more qualified people and fewer unskilled employees or vice versa? Could salary increases be curtailed without damage to morale and performance? Are your employees motivated? Are each-way communications good? Are staff properly trained?

- Heating and lighting: could costs be cut by a switch from electricity to gas? Is insulation adequate? Is the temperature too high? Is the heating on longer than necessary? Has a heating engineer reviewed the system?

- Stationery: is the use of telephones, fax and messengers controlled? Could stationery costs be reduced by using another supplier?

- Professional fees: could the work of accountants, solicitors, etc., be carried out in-house? Are you getting value for money from your professional advisers?

These are ways in which business management can be made more efficient. Other opportunities will open up, depending on your particular business. Matters of policy, which could effect the pattern of your business, are even more important. These include:

- Production: could benefits flow from new machinery or equipment? Would modern equipment lead to savings in terms of manpower and space? Would computerised machine tools improve productivity and quality?

- Marketing: could your sales force be reduced, with a consequent reduction in cars, travelling and other expenses? Are your sales and marketing techniques appropriate? Do you make use of corporate videos or direct mail? Do you use seminars?

- Advertising: advertising and public relations may impact on sales but not necessarily in the short term. Should your advertising programme be reduced or cut out altogether? Are there more direct ways of marketing? Bear in mind the fact that your customers are also seeking ways to reduce costs.

- Location: are your premises too large? Could you operate just as efficiently in less space or in a cheaper area, saving rent and business rates? Would the likely savings justify the cost of moving?

Such key decisions should only be made after preparing a mini-forecast to demonstrate the anticipated benefits. The temptation is to sack staff, cut advertising, restrict spending on new equipment and cancel research programmes. Action along these lines will improve profitability and cash flow in the short term but may do irreparable damage in the long term.

TRAINING

TRAINING FOR SUCCESS

Relatively few UK businesses are renowned for management training. Although some three million employees are involved in managerial roles in the UK – and 100,000 join the ranks each year – the majority of managers have no prior management education or training. Taking into account all UK managers, it is estimated that on average, one day each year is spent on management training.

Compared with other leading industrial countries such as the United States, Japan, West Germany and France, the UK has neglected training its managerial class. A report published by the National Economic Development Office suggests that the UK needs to devote nearly ten times as much effort to training if all would-be managers and executives are to be appropriately educated. They should also spend one week a year in off-the-job training.

These statistics relate to all businesses and it can be assumed that the situation among small firms is that much worse. By way of generalisation, proprietors of small businesses do not tend to see ongoing education in business as a priority. A recent study of UK entrepreneurs indicates that few saw any relationship between their academic qualifications and their business achievements.

Owner-managers tend to be disdainful of training which they perceive as an expensive luxury. Skill and knowledge may be required to develop the initial business idea but, when the business is up and running, the entrepreneur is often reluctant to undergo training and equally unwilling to allow managers and staff to do so. Put another way, entrepreneurs are so busy running their businesses that they don't have time for training and don't think they need it.

The hard-pressed businessman's perception is that his most precious resource is his time and if his business is proving a success he will probably get by without training.

But if such people can be enticed away from their businesses, their expertise can be developed. In the medium to long term their businesses would almost certainly benefit, and the reward could conceivably be the difference between continued growth and failure.

Business education should not be confused with management development. Business education is the basic knowledge and analytical skill which the individual should have acquired either before, or at the time of, entering business. Management development concerns the sharpening of the individual's skills so that he manages and develops his business to maximum potential. The most important elements of management development are:

● Management of people within and outside the business.

● Management of resources, finance and the operation of the business.

● Personal effectiveness: communication with people, contacts, motivation and self-awareness.

One of the owner-managers' major problems is learning how to delegate. Entrepreneurs are usually skilled in one aspect of the business − making or selling the product − but this is not the same as running a business. When the business starts to expand, the entrepreneur must manage and delegate; practices which do not necessarily come naturally.

Awareness of the need for management training has, of late, increased in the UK. Owner-managers must ensure that they take advantage of available programmes.

Many larger companies provide their own management training. The business departments of universities, polytechnics and colleges of further education often provide advice and management training. Various courses are available − during evenings or weekends − for individuals, or groups through their employers.

The Management Charter Initiative has drawn attention to, and emphasised the importance of, management training and development.

The Department of Employment recently set out four routes to growth which need to be better exploited:

• Large companies that purchase from SMEs, along with the accountancy and legal firms that provide advice, should share expertise and knowledge and act as a focus for training and local advisory services.

• There is more scope for small firms to set up or join their local Chamber of Commerce, business club, trade, profession or representative organisations. Such organisations can introduce outside expertise and advice and arrange training, on a variety of topics, on a cheaper and more cost-effective basis than individual firms.

• Business schools, consultants, professional institutes, Local Enterprise Agencies and other business organisations should explore more ways of marketing their services to SMEs – particularly those on the threshold of expansion.

• The Department of Employment's training and counselling services cater specifically for businessmen involved in the transition between start-up and a fully operational business. The DE, through the Training Agency, offers a range of training programmes. Marketed as 'Business Growth Training', the DE's programmes offer free kits and expert advice, low-cost seminars, subsidised consultancies, specialist advice for projects jointly produced with other businesses and financial help for innovative training.

Short courses on business skills are also available. Those who find themselves unemployed can turn to the Employment Training programme, while the Youth in Business Training programme beckons the young.

Some 80 business-led Training and Enterprise Councils (TECs) have been set up in the UK. TECs assume responsibility for the Training Agency's key role in training the young and the unemployed, along with its small firms programmes. A limited number of TECs take part in a pilot scheme to provide vocational training and education for those

16–19 year olds who receive 'Training Credits' on leaving school.

TECs represent a partnership between the private and public sectors and reflect the DE's philosophy that business training should become the responsibility of the local community.

There is a considerable choice of training programmes, and the problem for the owner-manager is to decide which is most appropriate. Advice should be sought from a relevant authority such as the local TEC, the DE, a polytechnic or a Chamber of Commerce.

The Training Agency has established Training Access Points (TAPs) which provide quick access to up-to-date information regarding training opportunities. Small businesses can use TAPs in local libraries or the TAP telephone service to identify suitable programmes.

What must be determined is whether a free or inexpensive off-the-peg course is appropriate or whether a tailor-made programme is required. What entrepreneurs should appreciate is that time and money invested in training will add to the success of a business and increase its value.

ALTERNATIVE FINANCE

ALL THE FUN OF THE FRANCHISE

The aspiring businessman might muse: 'Why not try a franchise?' He may not know precisely what is meant by the term 'franchise' but he will have heard of it and may believe that it will enable him to take advantage of a proven business idea, obtain all the help and support he needs from the franchisor, and end up with a substantial profit.

Similarly, a successful small-business operation may look at franchising as a way to expand its market – at relatively little cost – with the prospect of receiving fees and royalties from franchisees who utilise its business expertise.

Certainly, franchising is a fast-growing sector. The industry employs more than 250,000 people, more than half of whom would not have gone into business on their own were it not for franchising.

Franchising is an effective business system: it is relatively well regulated and is supported by the major clearing banks and other financial institutions. There are fewer business failures in franchising than elsewhere, although that is not to say the industry is failure-free. Far from it.

Let us define the term 'franchise'. Franchising can take place between manufacturer and retailer where the franchisee sells the product direct to the public – for example, car dealerships and petrol stations. There can be franchising between manufacturer and wholesaler where the franchisee is permitted to produce the product under licence – e.g. Coca-Cola.

And there can be franchises between wholesaler and retailer where there is a contract between a wholesaling organisation and a group of retailers with agreement as to pricing, merchandising and membership. Finally, there is the Business Format franchise – the arrangement which the term 'franchising' usually refers to.

The Business Format franchise involves a company or

individual (the franchisee) being granted a licence by a franchisor. This allows the franchisee to trade under the franchisor's name and benefit from the goodwill and marketing initiative of the franchisor. The package, which the franchisee buys, may include training and business advice.

A franchise is something more than an agency. The essential elements are listed by Martin Mendelsohn, a leading legal authority on franchising.

- There must be a contract containing all the terms agreed.

- The franchisor must initiate and train the franchisee in all aspects of the business and assist in its opening.

- The franchisee is permitted, under the control of the franchisor, to operate under a trade name, format and/or procedure, and with the benefit of goodwill owned by the franchisor.

- The franchisee must make a substantial capital investment from his own resouces.

- The franchisee must own his business.

- The franchisee pays the franchisor for the rights which he requires and for continuing services.

- The franchisee is given territory in which to operate.

Not all businesses are suitable for franchising. Most of the successful ones are in retailing and the provision of services – e.g. fast foods, home improvement, cleaning, printing, delivery services, hairdressing, fashion, equipment hire and estate agency.

It is, of course, possible for the expanding business to own certain outlets itself and allow franchisees to operate others.

Franchising, at its best, is a long-term partnership between franchisor and franchisee. Each party shares some of the risks and some of the profits.

Franchising may well appeal to those who want to break away from employment and start their own business but have no clear idea of the sort of business which will suit them best. Lack of technical knowledge is not a crucial factor because the franchisor will provide training, back-up support and a framework within which the business can be established.

It appeals to the more cautious because the investment is less than a normal start-up. The franchisor will have carried out the research and development to establish a product or service for which a market already exists.

Meanwhile, the franchisor will be at pains to ensure that he selects the right people because the success of the franchise depends on their achievements.

The franchisee needs many of an entrepreneur's attributes and also an ability and willingness to operate the system laid down by the franchisor. He must also believe in the product or service.

Alan Foxwell, a colleague at Touche Ross, sums up the case for taking out a franchise: 'The risks involved in starting up a business are reduced. But there is a price to pay for the franchisor's name and expertise. Their worth needs to be carefully considered when projecting the profits you will receive from your business. It is usually a case of less risk, less profit.'

Anyone taking on a franchise needs to obtain detailed information about the franchisor: its business and track record. A copy of the last accounts should be scrutinised by an accountant.

It is advisable to sound out existing franchisees. The franchisor may offer to make introductions but independent inquiries will not go amiss.

You should take advice from your solicitor and particularly your accountant but remember: only you can satisfy yourself that the franchise offers you a long-term business relationship.

These are some questions you should ask:

- Will the franchisor find and negotiate a site for you?

- Will you buy or lease the equipment necessary to operate the business and how often will you be expected to re-equip or refit the premises?

- What is the total cost of establishing the business and what is included in the way of ongoing franchise fees or royalties?

- What initial services will the franchisor provide, such as support staff and an opening launch?

- What training facilities are provided, initially and in the future?

- What support will the franchisor give in terms of advertising and promotion? How much will you have to contribute?

- What level of gross profit margin can you expect to achieve?

- What expenses are you likely to incur and what is the level of turnover required to break even?

- Does the franchisor take a mark-up on goods and services provided and, if so, what protection do you have against unfair and unjustified price increases? Do you have to take a minimum amount of goods and services from the franchisor and, if so, how is this calculated and what happens if you fail to meet the commitment?

- Will you be provided with ongoing research and development, marketing and business advice? Can you negotiate bulk purchasing terms?

- What is the likely life span of the product or service provided?

- Can you be confident that the product or service will be developed and updated?

From the franchisor's point of view, franchising offers the opportunity of more rapid expansion with lower capital investment and less risk.

The franchise agreement should ensure the franchisee's commitment and reduce administration costs. Other advantages should include economies of scale in purchasing goods and the opportunity to pass on advertising and public relations expenses. On the other hand, there will be less profit and less control over the business than if the franchisor ran it himself.

The franchisee is offered the opportunity to set up and run his own business with the advantages and economies of scale of a large organisation. He enjoys the benefits of a proven product, professional management advice and marketing and promotional campaigns. He can expect assistance in respect of site selection and business layout. He benefits from the franchisor's know-how and business research.

On the other hand, the conduct of the business is, to a greater or lesser extent, regulated by the franchisor. The franchisee is dependent on the service provided by the franchisor. He may feel that the business is not really his own and that he is acting as a manager for the franchisor. While it is true that he takes less risk, there is a price to pay for the franchise package: sharing profits with the franchisor.

Franchises: How to Cut a Fair Deal

As I have already stressed, most franchises relate to retailing and services. The cost of purchasing a franchise varies enormously – from a few thousand pounds to more than £1 million.

Some typical examples are £6000 for a Photomaid franchise; £12,500 for Complete Weed Control; £21,000 for Dyno-Rod; £25,000 for Avis Rent A Car; £85,000 for Chicken George (American fried chicken); and £1 million for a Holiday Inn.

Not that the initial fee is the be-all and end-all in terms of start-up costs. There are also capital costs, such as building work, equipment, shop fittings and vehicles. Clearly the expense will be greater if the business requires High Street frontage and if the shop layout and window-dressing is in 'house' style.

There will almost certainly be ongoing commitments to pay royalties, to make contributions towards expenditure incurred by the franchisor and to spend money under various headings set out in the franchise agreement, such as architects' fees, maintenance and training. Finally, there will be a requirement for working capital, the amount of which will depend on the type of business and, in particular, whether it is one which involves funds being tied up in stock and debtors.

Franchising is a business format favoured by the major banks, so the purchase price of the franchise and the capital costs may be financed via a bank loan, providing, of course, that the bank is satisfied with the business, its management and with the suggested product or service.

Banks should be prepared to lend approximately two-thirds of the costs – where the franchisor and franchisee are approved – perhaps more if the viability study and business plan are impressive.

One of the reasons why banks are prepared to lend to franchise businesses is that they enjoy a much higher success rate than the average start-up. Many small firms go under during the first five years because what appeared to be a good idea in theory proved not so good in practice. All the major clearing banks have formed franchise units to deal with the special requirements of franchising.

Before you start up a franchise business you should carry out a viability study to ascertain whether the franchisor's proposals are acceptable and the forecasts realistic. You may well think: 'If this is really such a good idea, why isn't the owner exploiting it himself?' This is why you need to produce a business plan which will not differ materially from that prepared for any other business start-up.

First of all, you need to satisfy yourself that you are cut out to run a franchising business. Remember that you will be restricted to some extent by the fact that the business is a franchise and you will be bound by the terms of the franchisor's agreement. Technical expertise may not be essential, but loyalty to the franchisor, commitment to the business idea and a willingness to work long hours need to be fully demonstrated.

Forecasts for a franchising business are somewhat easier to prepare than for an ordinary start-up because you can draw on the experience of other franchisees. You will be selling a proven product or service, so income estimates should be more certain and various expenditure items will be determined by the franchising agreement.

One factor which the franchisee should bear in mind is that he will require funds to meet living costs while the business is being established. Experience shows that a build up of sales usually takes longer than expected. Because cash flow is critical to a franchising business, it is prudent to prepare forecasts on the basis that delays can be expected. It is important to be flexible when you calculate how much you need to borrow. Carry out a sensitivity analysis – ask yourself questions that begin: 'What if . . .?'

If an existing business plans to expand its products or services through franchising, the considerations will be different. What must be fully appreciated is that the success of the franchisor depends on the success of the franchisee. There is only one cake to be cut and each party wants a fair slice.

A key point in the franchisor's business plan should be the strength of his management team. Is there sufficient management depth to cope with the additional responsibilities of setting up, launching, administering and controlling a group of franchisees?

You must also ensure that your income flow is sufficient to meet the cost of starting up new franchises, along with the training and supervision of franchisees. A common fault is to underestimate the time it takes to get a franchise programme up and running. Expect your cash-flow forecast to show the need for additional finance when the franchisees are building up to optimum activity.

The final stage is to complete the franchise agreement. Legal advice should be obtained to ensure that the terms are acceptable. Model agreements are available which will include clauses which deal with:

- The amount to be paid for the purchase of the franchise.

- The services to be provided by the franchisor in respect of site plans; conversion and refurbishment, equipment, training, launch support, merchandising, advertising, public relations and procedure manuals.

- Restrictions on competition and running other businesses.

- The term of the agreement and arrangements for renewal.

- Arrangements for use of the name, trade mark, logos, etc.

- Arrangements for termination of the agreement.

- Provision for the payments of royalties or additional fees.

- Requirements regarding standards and the uniformity of business procedures.

- Insurance requirements.

There are many other matters to be dealt with before opening shop, such as production of a sales brochure, agreement over an advertising and public relations programme, finalisation of an operations manual, stationery design and training.

Franchising, by way of generalisation, is a well-organised industry and a considerable amount of advice is available. The British Franchising Association's major aim is to sort out the good franchisors from the bad and set standards.

Local Enterprise Agencies are eager to advise on start-ups and will be familiar with local problems. Details of the clearing banks' franchise units are available from high-street branches.

Many firms of solicitors specialise in franchising and, similarly, many firms of chartered accountants can offer guidance, particularly in respect of your business plan.

BUYING A BUSINESS FROM THE RECEIVER

An entrepreneur or owner-manager does not have to start a business from scratch. Many opportunities exist to buy companies which are up and running, even well established.

One source of ready-made and often successful businesses is the receiver. It may be that a receiver is selling an entire business, or the profitable subsidiaries of an insolvent group which ran into financial difficulties.

The purchaser in such situations could be a management team intent on acquiring a substantial stake – perhaps even 100 per cent – of the business, in the expectation that once the existing structure is removed, performance will improve. A process better known as a management buy-out (MBO).

It may be that the purchasers are outsiders who believe that a new management team will stimulate performance, in other words a management buy-in (MBI). Or the purchasers may be a combination of the two groups, with the existing management team strengthened by certain outsiders who have specific knowledge and skills.

The fact that an administrative receiver is involved does not mean that the business is not viable. New management, corporate restructuring or a cash injection may make the business flourish as never before. Extricating the business from an insolvent structure may be all that is needed.

Venture capitalists may be prepared to back the MBO or MBI team because the business has a track record – with an established product or service – and, in the case of an MBO, the relevant knowledge and experience. Similarly, the clearing banks are likely to make loans and overdrafts available to the team because there is less risk of failure than in a start-up.

With an increasing number of companies under pressure, opportunities exist for entrepreneurs to diversify and expand at relatively low cost.

An administrative receiver may seek to sell a business subsidiary for various reasons: it may not fit into the group's structure; it may require considerable investment in terms of cash or management time; it may be in the wrong location; or it may be making losses.

A common problem is that the management lacks vision – a factor which may encourage an MBI team to grasp the opportunity to turn the business round and expand it.

The vital ingredients are a capable group of managers and a financial structure which allows a reasonable burden of debt and finance charges to be absorbed.

There are several advantages to buying from a receiver:

- The receiver will usually want to agree and complete a deal quickly, often within eight weeks.

- There is the flexibility to select only the assets required.

- The purchaser may be able to select the executives and employees whom he wishes to employ.

- The receiver has obligations to those who appoint him. He must maximise realisations and he has a duty of care. But he will want a straightforward deal with the maximum amount of cash up front. If the purchaser is prepared to accept some of the liabilities to employees, a reduction in purchase price is possible.

There are other matters which the buying team should take into account:

- Are there any third-party claims based on retention of title to the assets which are being acquired?

- Can a discount or charge be made for collecting debts which are taken over?

- Are there any relevant patents or intellectual property which can be acquired for a small addition to the purchase price?

- Are there any leases or hire-purchase arrangements? If so, it may be better to negotiate direct with the finance house rather than the receiver.

• Since no warranties or indemnities are likely to be forthcoming, it is essential to take legal advice from a firm which is familiar with this market. There is a limit to what can be negotiated with a receiver as he is answerable to others.

• Can part of the purchase price be retained until the transaction is completed and all the assets are physically acquired?

• Ensure that the assets are unencumbered.

• There may be scope to allocate the purchase price in a tax efficient way: for example, attribute full value to stock, debtors, and so on, for immediate tax relief. Attribute value to assets which qualify for capital allowances, such as plant and motor vehicles. Finally, put as little value as can be justified on intangible assets such as goodwill and intellectual property.

MBOs and MBIs have averaged 450 per annum for the last four years and now account for a significant proportion of all merger and acquisition activity. The current economic climate and high interest rates can prove a hostile environment for management teams. But, with care, there are bargains to be found.

Chris Ward, corporate finance partner with Touche Ross, recently set out ten tips for a successful MBO from a receiver:

• Speed: act quickly, the receiver will.

• Independent financial advice: appoint an experienced adviser to conduct negotiations with the receiver and the financial backers.

• Legal advice: appoint a reputable commercial firm with insolvency experience which will not waste time seeking warranties and indemnities which a receiver will not give.

- Management team: the team must cover all relevant business skills, particularly financial.

- Strategy: have a long-term plan which focuses on how, and in which direction, your business will grow. This is an opportunity not a millstone.

- Assets: aim to purchase only those assets which are needed for the business but have regard to what the receiver wants out of the deal. He will usually prefer to sell all assets to one purchaser and this will give scope for price negotiation.

- Reorganisation costs: calculate the maximum liability, including redundancy costs, and take these into account in the offer price.

- Financial structure: your financial plan should make adequate provision for the purchase and working capital needed to expand the business.

- Consideration: see if part of the consideration can be retained to cover unforseen liabilities.

- Keep it simple: the receiver will find it difficult to resist a neat package.

FACTORING

Factoring is often seen as an alternative to liquidation or receivership for companies with cash problems. But, while factoring can be a useful source of capital for growing businesses, it is almost certainly not the answer if a company has failed.

Factors provide three basic services for customer businesses:

- Sales-ledger administration, which includes credit control, issue of invoices and statements as agreed with the customer and debt collection.

- Finance: factors usually advance 80–85 per cent of an issued invoice's value, with the balance, less interest and administration costs, payable when the invoice is settled.

- Bad-debt protection can be offered on a non-recourse basis so that customers have total protection against bad debts on approved sales. This service incurs a higher charge.

With the number of receiverships running at record levels, factoring and invoice-discounting services remain popular. There has been a significant increase in the companies which use factoring and the value of invoices discounted continues to grow.

Gordon Harris, director of sales and marketing of Griffin Factors, informs me that factoring business overall rose 15 per cent in 1990 to £13.8 billion, with the debt-discounting element accounting for £7.2 billion – up 20 per cent. The major factors absorbed some £11.9 million in bad debts, compared with just over £5 million in 1989.

During the 1980s factoring, and in particular debt-discounting, became more widely accepted as a source of working capital for small expanding businesses.

One reason is that the range of finance on offer for such

companies is limited. Loans can be unsuitable as working capital and usually require a charge on assets, often property. Small amounts of venture capital have always been in short supply and banks have their limitations.

At its simplest, factoring allows a business to make maximum use of one of its largest assets: unpaid debts. The average business is likely to have at least two months' sales – some 20 per cent of annual turnover – tied up in debt at any time.

If such debts are discounted and 80 per cent of their value released, the need for a bank overdraft or medium-term borrowing is reduced. Such improved cash flow can enable the business to pay customers more quickly, with the advantage of discounts for cash or quantity, and mean an improved credit rating. It is debt-discounting which provides factoring's essential appeal.

Other aspects of factoring should not be ignored. A business which is starting up or in the early stages of development can save time and costs if sales-ledger administration is passed to the factor.

Factors will administer credit control, check out new customers, issue invoices and collect debts in an efficient way, which may be impossible for a young business where office procedures are not the top priority. Factors can manage the sales ledger better and collect debts quicker than is otherwise possible.

Companies may want to refer to their sales ledgers even after control has been transferred to the factor. Very often this can be done by plugging into the factor's on-line computer system.

Invoice-discounting can be adapted to particular businesses – for example, there may be one or two large reliable customers who always pay on time, but to receive up to 90 per cent of the amount due a month earlier would improve cash flow. Invoice-discounting can help iron out the peaks and troughs of seasonal trade or occasional large orders.

Similarly, the bad-debt-protection service can take various forms apart from pure insurance. Factors can run local credit management in overseas markets for exporters, keep sales-ledger records and arrange finance in overseas currencies.

Such services can be of considerable benefit to new exporters, allowing competition on equal terms with overseas competitors.

Debt-discounting services can be provided on a confidential basis so that customers do not realise they are dealing with a factor.

Most leading UK factors and discounters are owned by the major banks and are members of the Association of British Factors and Discounters. There are 11 companies in this category which account for some 90 per cent of the market. The other 10 per cent are members of the Association of Invoice Factors and numerous independents. There is a belief that factoring is expensive, but if the costs and interest saved are taken into account it can prove a saving. The costs falls into two categories:

- Service charges: these depend on the number and average value of invoices, the type of business and the nature of the service provided. The charge for sales-ledger administration is more than for discounting. A debt protection service means a further charge – depending on whether a recourse or non-recourse basis is used. Charges are usually between one and three per cent of invoices handled. Since terms are negotiable it may be worth comparing factors.

- Interest: linked to bank base rates, interest will be charged in respect of the advance made on discounted invoices. Factors invariably charge a lower rate than applies to the customers' bank overdraft. There will not be any arrangement fee, as is charged on loans or overdrafts by the banks.

While a three per cent charge on annual turnover may seem excessive, perhaps it is reasonable when the cost of sales-ledger administration, credit controllers, cash-flow monitoring, computer software, telephone calls and other such administrative costs – add to these bad debts if the 'no recourse' debt-protection service is used – are taken into account.

Factoring cannot be considered in isolation. It is just one

element of business finance which must be linked with bank facilities. Banks are likely to restrict their facilities if debts are factored because security will be reduced. But if bank facilities are already restricted, it may be possible to include debt-discounting as a source of finance without any further reduction in the bank facility. It is subject to negotiation and, bearing in mind that most major factors are owned by the clearing banks, it may be a matter of choosing the right factor.

The arrangement between factor and customer will be subject to an agreement. There are certain points which the customer should check:

- Are there any restrictions on the invoices which may be discounted? Are all goods and services to all customers included? Are there any conditions which apply to new customers? Are there limits on the size of invoice or the volume of business in any one month?

- Will advances be made in respect of invoices as they are issued? Is the advance the maximum which can be obtained – 80 or perhaps 85 per cent?

- Will interest or discount be charged at a rate which compares favourably with a bank overdraft? Will it be simple or compound interest?

- Are any personal guarantees required from the business owners or other companies associated with them?

- Are requirements as to the recourse or non-recourse debt-protection service, and disclosed or non-disclosed use of factor, being observed?

- Is there a conflict with the bank?

- Good communication between factor and customer is essential. A specific person in the factor's office should be responsible for each customer.

Factoring should be planned in advance with terms agreed when the business is in good shape. Factors, like most other institutions, will not want to know when a business is in trouble.

MARKETING

MARKETING

Business failures are often blamed on bad marketing but, more often than not, a business fails because the owners misjudged the market: sales fall short of expectations and cash-flow problems follow. Many small businesses fold because the owners believed that their product or service was just what the public wanted, the only problem being how to supply whatever in sufficient quantities. The reality was that the goods or services were not just what the public wanted.

Marketing is all about providing the right goods or services to the right customers at the right price.

Marketing is a term often used without any real understanding of what it means. Many directors perceive marketing as a secondary activity which can be delegated, and not a few labour under the impression that the function is little more than a grandiose term for corporate hospitality – at home and abroad.

This, of course, is far from the truth. Small firms, whether in the process of starting up or developing new markets and products, cannot afford to ignore marketing: it is critical to business success.

Marketing is no easy task. Research has to be carried out and the results analysed. A SWOT analysis (Strengths, Weaknesses, Opportunities and Threats) can be used to set out the options, determine the strategies and agree specific courses of action.

Most new businesses are formed because their owners believe they have identified a gap in the market for a product or service. The art is to turn such a hunch into a successful business.

Entrepreneurs starting up in business should not see marketing as a one-off exercise. It is a continuous and evolving process which should be regularly monitored, updated and developed. Basic elements are:

- The market: Define the market and its prospects.
  Identify a specific market niche in terms of product, area and customers: this will mean dividing the market into segments.

- Customers: Prepare customer profiles: who are they, where are they, when do they buy, who decides to buy?
  Is there a small number of key customers or a wide spread with no dominant group?
  The product or service must be critically examined from the customer's perspective.

- Competition: Assess the competition: where they operate, their size, market share and potential.
  Examine competitors' strengths and weaknesses.
  Is there room for competition?

- The business: What are your territorial objectives? Is your market the UK, the EC or international?
  A pricing policy must be drawn up: is the business to be cost or demand based? It is essential to demonstrate that your pricing policy allows market penetration, while yielding a healthy profit.
  Support and after-sales service and warranty arrangements must be considered.
  The minimum size of orders along with credit terms must be determined.
  Distribution is a key consideration.

The answers to such questions require research which many small firms do not have the resources or skills to conduct. Outside consultants may have to be brought in. Once all the information has been assembled the findings must be analysed. Once again, use the SWOT formula.

A number of options for marketing the product or service will emerge. A review and costing of such options should be included in the overall business plan and a marketing strategy drawn up.

This strategy should encompass: products and services, target customers, pricing structure, distribution arrangements and back-up services.

The object of the exercise is to establish that a market exists for the product or service which can be sold in sufficient quantities – correctly priced – to ensure a profit in line with business plan forecasts.

It may be that insufficient information is available to make a simple choice of possible options. This is when the entrepreneur's vision plays a vital role. The success of many businesses relates as much to entrepreneurial flair as research and analysis.

With any enterprise the essence of marketing success relates to the judicious balance between the creative and visionary elements and research and analysis.

Either way a marketing strategy, which sets out detailed plans for the forthcoming year and outline plans for the subsequent two years, is required.

Responsibilities for implementation should be assigned to specific members of staff. Estimate costs and set benchmarks against which performance can be measured.

Communications are an essential aspect of marketing and include:

- Promotional material for each market sector, such as brochures, catalogues and packaging: all in corporate style.

- Meeting and entertaining major customers and prospective customers.

- Exhibitions and seminars.

- Media activities such as newspaper articles.

- Advertising focused on specific products and services. Be mindful of costs.

- Public relations, including press releases and sponsorship.

Some businessmen find that marketing comes naturally and encounter little difficulty in working out a programme. Others find marketing hard work and take the view that the effort entailed in research and analysis is better channelled into more tangible areas. Those who harbour such views tend to rely on external advisers.

A great deal has been written on the subject of marketing, the difficulty being how to adapt such general advice to a specific business.

The Department of Employment's Small Firms' Service, Local Enterprise Agencies and the British Overseas Trade Board are useful ports of call.

The Department of Trade and Industry's Enterprise Initiative offers a marketing consultancy. Designed for firms with less than 500 employees, the consultancy concentrates on customer requirements, marketing strategies and the development of export markets.

Part of the package is a free two-day business review carried out by a DTI enterprise counsellor who will advise on growth prospects and the relevance of consultancy advice.

The DTI counsellor may suggest the appointment of a professional firm of consultants whose review could take three working weeks. Half the cost of such a consultancy is usually met by the DTI.

The Department of Employment recently launched the Small Business Training Programme. This comprises 25 independent modules, priced at £105 each, plus VAT. Four of the modules are particularly relevant: marketing; developing products and services; advertising and promotion; and selling.

Advice is available from the Institute of Marketing, various trade associations and numerous firms which specialise in advertising, public relations and marketing.

Independent consultants can be called upon to carry out research and analysis and advise on marketing strategy. Major accountancy firms offer such services through their respective management-consultancy offshoots.

I have set out what might loosely be termed the rules of marketing but there are many instances where such rules have been broken – with considerable success.

The Sony Walkman received a thumbs down in terms of market research – findings which were sensibly ignored by Akio Morita, one of Sony's founders. Alan Sugar's instincts were primarily responsible for the success of the Amstrad word processor. In contrast, Sir Clive Sinclair's C5 vehicle, popularly known as the electric clog, proved a disaster.

Generally speaking, it is best to stick to familiar markets and develop greater expertise; do not dabble or diversify in an attempt to solve problems and do not try to outguess established rivals.

If you choose to break the rules, it is best to do so in your own backyard, as Sugar did with consumer products, rather than in someone else's, as Sinclair attempted with automobiles.

YOU AND 1992

A survey carried out by Graham Bannock and Partners on behalf of the National Westminster Bank revealed that only one in four small businesses in the UK have made any preparations for the Single Market in 1992. It would appear that as many as 85 per cent of firms surveyed have considered the implications but only 33 per cent see more opportunities for exports after 1992. Some 56 per cent of those surveyed either believe that the Single Market will not affect them or do not know whether it will or not.

Reasons for this apparent apathy included a lack of information – despite the considerable efforts of the British Overseas Trade Board (BOTB) – and two other somewhat feeble excuses: 'We do not believe we are affected' and 'We want to wait and see what happens first.' Other problems embraced lack of market research, nervousness about conducting business in foreign-language-speaking countries, uncertainties about financing such business development and apprehension regarding export documentation.

It is generally recognised that 1992 will open up new markets, herald freer trade within the European Economic Community and present many, albeit not all, companies with opportunities for expansion.

Yet 56 per cent of the small-business community still believes the Single Market will not affect them, while only nine per cent think they will suffer from increased competition: possibly because they have not thought the issue through. It is interesting to note that awareness of the threat of overseas competition in the home market appears to increase in line with the size of companies surveyed.

Small businesses would be well advised to pay more attention to export markets in general and Europe in particular. Excuses such as: 'I cannot obtain the information' or 'It does not really affect us' hardly hold water, particularly in view of the comprehensive booklets provided by the Department of Trade and Industry through BOTB.

A businessman who is intent on overseas expansion should obtain a copy of *The Export Initiative: A Guide to Exporting*, from one of BOTB's regional offices. To simplify matters, telephone the '1992 Hotline': 081–200 1992.

BOTB's objective is to encourage those who have no experience of overseas trading to examine their export potential, while also encouraging the experienced exporter to improve performance. In both instances, advice and practical help are readily available.

It is not only major companies that export profitably; on the contrary small companies represent some of our most successful exporters. Small businesses often benefit from faster decision-making processes, more flexible production schedules and direct personal contact between those running the business and overseas customers.

Should you decide to start exporting for the first time, you should bear in mind the practical advice and 'hand-holding' service provided by the national network of Export Development Advisers, available through the BOTB's regional offices. As with all business enterprises, a business plan is required. You may already have the staff and expertise available to plan and develop an export marketing strategy. But not all small businesses can afford the dedicated management time required and may benefit from the professional advice available under the DTI Enterprise Initiative.

The DTI Enterprise Initiative offers businesses which employ fewer than 500 people access to independent professional advice, designed to develop management skills in areas crucial to success at home and overseas. Expert consultancy advice is available in six different areas: marketing (including export marketing), design, quality, manufacturing systems, business planning and financial and information systems. The DTI funds half the cost of between five and 15 consultant days. Before the consultancy starts, companies receive a free 'business review' carried out by a DTI Enterprise Counsellor. It may be that such an initiative will prompt an ambitious company to cross the English Channel and become a successful exporter.

You must be satisfied that selling overseas is the right way for your company to progress. Exporting requires commitment, patience, resources and expertise. These are some of the questions you must ask yourself:

- What additional financing will be required and is it available?

- What sort of return and positive cash flow is required from export operations?

- Does the business have the management resources to expand abroad?

- Is there a market for the products at the right price?

- Will the quality of the products match the competition?

- Do the products match up to EEC requirements, particularly in the context of environment and pollution control?

- What training will be necessary in respect of foreign languages, dealing with foreign currencies, documentation, etc.

Obviously you have to decide precisely which markets to tackle. Visiting the market can prove a valuable aspect of research but much of the information required – such as the size of the market, the likely demand for your products, local and international competition, political and economic stability, import restrictions and technical standards – will be available in the UK.

Next, you must ascertain how best to establish a presence in the market. Studying the activities of your competitors should prove rewarding. Can you afford the management time necessary to maintain a direct relationship with customers? Or should you appoint someone to represent you? How will you promote your product? Do you need to revise your sales literature and packaging to suit overseas customers?

Then come the nuts and bolts of the exporting process? How will your products be priced and how will they be delivered? Who will deal with the documentation? Can you make insurance arrangements to protect yourself against the buyer's default or other credit risks? If credit terms are for more than 30 days, can this be absorbed in your cash-flow projection?

It is imperative that your product is right for the market selected and it will be necessary to carry out research to ensure the demand exists. Market research is often cited as an obstacle to exporting, but BOTB possesses an Information Service Database and Information Centre which can provide information on products and markets, overseas agents and distributors and export opportunities, as well as statistics, market research reports, and overseas directories.

The Export Intelligence Service takes this a stage further, building up a database from Diplomatic Service posts throughout the world, indicating specific sales leads and pointers to future openings in various markets. This can be made available on line for use on a personal computer. If more structured market research is required, you will be put in touch with a professional adviser which may lead to a market survey, for which a grant may be applicable. BOTB fully recognises the importance of market research and has devoted considerable resources to this area. Charges are made for certain specialist services.

Despite the benefit of market research available in the UK, you will have to visit the target market to talk to potential customers and business representatives. This should help you determine the extent of local problems such as taxes, tariffs, regulations affecting UK exporters, etc.

You may decide to sell through a UK Export Agency but the more likely course is the appointment of an agent or distributor in the target country. The agent will not only have to sell your product but should also provide you with information which relates to your business, the market, and product promotion. This is a key appointment – an area in which BOTB can help by drawing on its Diplomatic Service data. You can, of course, advertise and make contacts at trade fairs, etc., but it is essential to meet your representative in his own territory.

Once a good representative is in place, you must keep in touch. One cost-effective way of doing this is by attending overseas trade fairs, perhaps even taking a stand. An organisation called the Simpler Trade Procedures Board (SITPRO) can advise on how to cut down the red tape and reduce paperwork in respect of exports. A list of specialists in export documentation is available which is particularly useful to those unfamiliar with procedures. Remember: mistakes in documents are often responsible for hold ups in the movement of goods and money.

It is vitally important to ensure that goods are delivered to their destination on time. A small business would probably be well advised to appoint a freight-forwarding and shipping company to assume responsibility for the entire operation: transport, documentation, customs clearance and insurance.

Prompt payment and the avoidance of bad debts are also key considerations.

Overseas customers are not necessarily slow payers but it must be recognised that credit risks exist in every market. Apart from buyer default, the exporter has to contend with other factors such as exchange controls, political risks, even war – all of which can prevent payment. Credit insurance cover can be taken out through the Export Credit Guarantee Department (ECGD). This will insure you against default, insolvency, restriction on remittances, cancellation of licences, etc. Normally, you can insure 90 per cent of the risk, either on export sales in entirety or in part. It is also possible to negotiate one-off deals in respect of individual export orders. An ECGD policy can be used as security for obtaining payment in advance from the bank. ECGD Insurance Services can be contacted through BOTB's regional offices.

Exporting is obviously hard work, but it may be the initiative your company should take if it is seeking to expand. If your business faces increased competition from overseas, it may be essential.

TOUGH TIMES

WHY FIRMS GO BUST

A record 24,442 businesses failed during 1990 – the highest total for a decade – and all the indications are that a significantly greater number of firms will go to the wall this year.

According to Dun & Bradstreet, the business information specialists, last year's failures showed a 35 per cent increase compared with 1989.

This means that company failures – liquidations plus bankruptcies – are running at more than twice the level of 1980, the first full year of Mrs Thatcher's tenure.

In 1980 the number of collapses totalled 10,651. This figure rose steadily to reach 21,682 in 1984. In 1989, 18,163 businesses went under.

Last year's wave of failures reflects the impact of the recession in terms of the rapid decline in consumer and business demand. The collapses involved close on 14,000 liquidations and almost 11,000 bankruptcies with London and the south-east accounting for well nigh half the companies that succumbed to the recession.

My colleague Christopher Morris, who specialises in liquidations, reports that the trend has continued well into 1991.

High interest rates, the impact of the Uniform Business Rate and spiralling salary costs will, inevitably, take their toll.

The message from Morris, however, is: 'The banks are now much more sophisticated in dealing with problem lending. An early approach to the bank for help or advice can make all the difference between survival and failure.'

If you ask someone whose business has become insolvent, gone into liquidation or just faded away 'What happened? What went wrong?', he is likely to say: 'We ran out of money.' If pressed, he might well add: 'There really wasn't a market for our goods, our debtors wouldn't pay up, the competition was far too hot and the business was not very well situated. We were also under-capitalised and staff costs were just too high.'

In most cases, such responses are cover-ups for bad management. Business failure usually reflects the failure of management to plan or take action which might have prevented failure.

Owner-manager failures fall under four main headings:

- Incompetence: no basic knowledge and skills to plan, manage and control the business.

- Lack of management experience: not enough experience in supervising employees and the work they do.

- Unbalanced experience: considerable formal education, but little or no practical experience of the particular industry in which they have chosen to operate.

- Personal weaknesses: the entrepreneur may not be cut out to run his own business. He may fail to make contacts or have difficulty in communicating with people, organising and motivating employees and adjusting to the realities of a business that may prove less attractive than anticipated.

Business difficulties are often reflected in alcoholism, breakdowns and marital problems. Running a venture tends to consume the entrepreneur's energies, emotions and time; he has little to give elsewhere and other commitments often suffer.

He may lose (or may never have had) the commitment and perseverance essential for running a successful and prosperous business.

The entrepreneur must be aware of the weaknesses which can cause a business to fail. He must acknowledge and understand the risks involved in running a business which, if not properly managed, may bring about his downfall.

Lack of professional advice

Cash is a limiting factor for many entrepreneurs, and they are often conspicuously slow to seek advice from accountants, marketing consultants and others because they consider it expensive and unnecessary. Many tend to rely heavily on informal business contacts whose advice may lead to bad decisions. There is a natural reluctance to seek advice after mistakes have been made. The time for advice is before making mistakes.

Inadequate financial resources

A business may fail if there are insufficient capital and loan facilities or a wrong mix of finance (for example, too much loan capital with interest charges which cannot be absorbed). Or available resources may have been exhausted on property, expensive equipment and cars without making sufficient provision for day-to-day working capital.

An initially viable financial plan may become untenable if there is overtrading or a delay in building up the business.

Lack of financial management and discipline

Financial control depends on accurate information about cash flow, profits and costs.

If there is no regular financial monitoring, inefficient or improper use of available resources may result.

Poor decision-making and planning

Many owner-managers do not plan ahead. Problems are dealt with on a day-to-day basis and no decisions — or the wrong decisions — are made. Such managers have not learned to delegate responsibility, nor has time and money been spent on training. Although ill-qualified, they attempt to do everything themselves.

Lack of technical skills

A poor product or service – possibly produced at an uncompetitive price – can reflect inadequate or out-of-date technology or untrained staff.

Poor marketing research and strategy

More business failures are attributed to sales and marketing than to administration.

Some so-called businesses never have a hope of success; they may be the founder's hobby, there may be no demand for the product or it may be impossible to produce it at a competitive price. The market may be notorious for bad debts or extended credit terms.

Expansion without planning

Entrepreneurs possess an inbuilt urge to expand, but often fail to appreciate that expansion requires careful planning. Symptoms usually include an inability to match production of goods or services with sales, excessive demands on cash resources, a breakdown of accounting and over-extended management.

Expansion may serve to highlight latent weaknesses, such as the failure to delegate or the failure to exercise proper financial control.

Wrong location

Cheap premises in the wrong area may prove a false economy, resulting in higher transport costs and staff shortages. On the other hand, many businesses have moved from a modest railway arch to larger, grander premises, only to fail.

Some of these causes of failure are more important than others.

Under-capitalisation, managerial incompetence and personality defects are prime causes and cannot usually be compensated for by other assets or plus factors.

Adequate finance and managerial competence are essential

but they must be supplemented by motivation, hard work, persistence and flexibility. Not to forget a good product or an innovative idea.

BANKS AND THE RECESSION

At the time of writing, rumours continue to circulate that the clearing banks are adopting a hard line and squeezing small businesses.

The popular view is that the Big Five are intent on reducing small companies' overdraft facilities and, in certain instances, have withdrawn facilities without warning. Many such tales have been exaggerated and, naturally enough, represent the customer's perspective.

Banks always review a business's requirements, its forecasts, its ability to repay and security, before a loan or overdraft facility is agreed. Time limits are usually placed on such facilities and a review carried out before renewal.

What is now becoming apparent is that many businesses which were viable a year ago are no longer so.

In such circumstances the banks, not surprisingly, want to limit or reduce their exposure. By and large, the banks try to achieve this in a reasonable manner but, inevitably, there will be instances when the owner-manager is confident that the business can survive the recession and emerge as a profitable enterprise – a view which may differ widely from that of his bank manager. Should the bank pull the rug, the entrepreneur's natural reaction is that the bank has acted unreasonably.

In the current climate the banks are well aware that they must monitor their small-business accounts regularly. Six-monthly reviews are no longer sufficient. A business which appears to be surviving one week may, within a matter of days, encounter a major bad debt or lose a large order – factors which can quickly lead to insolvency and wrongful trading. In such circumstances the banks must act quickly.

As Richard Cracknell, Barclays' senior business development manager, put it to me: 'The worrying factor is the speed with which businesses are failing in this current trough.'

Barclays, along with Lloyds, Midland and NatWest, insist that their loans managers have not been advised to limit the facilities available to small businesses. At the same time, all the High Street banks are monitoring business plans more strictly.

Stuart White, Midland Bank's enterprise sales manager, recently insisted that procedures have not changed. He stressed that the bank manager's role is to establish the key risk areas, assess such risks, and cover them by taking security, adjusting the interest rate and ensuring proper communication so that the situation can be monitored.

It is no secret that the clearing banks have suffered an increase in bad debts in respect of small businesses. Barclays are of the opinion that the bad-debt problem is worse in the South and South-east, while managers in the Midlands and the North are somewhat more optimistic about the future. Bankers take the view that bad debts do not necessarily reflect incorrect assessments of risk when the loans were first agreed. They attribute the problem to the recession.

The clearing banks emphasise they are still looking for worthwhile propositions. Indeed, some are still advertising the services they offer small businesses – including start-ups.

Paul Garland, Lloyds' deputy chief manager of commercial banking, informed me: 'All lending propositions must meet our quality requirements and the most important of these is the ability to repay. The ability of a company to generate cash, the life-blood of any business, is paramount at present.'

Barclays points out that property is still a sector with a health warning. Although property can be valued for security purposes, the problem is how to sell, should the need arise.

Despite this, anything between 7000 and 10,000 new businesses are starting up each week with NatWest claiming 30 per cent of the business and Barclays only just behind.

Lending to established businesses still shows a net increase. Cracknell's view is: 'If a troubled business can see light at the end of the tunnel an increase in facilities may see the company through its problems.'

Garland adds: 'No one, least of all bank managers, likes to see a small business in difficulty. Still less do we want to pull the plug on a struggling venture.'

Andy Hunter, NatWest's senior business development manager, stresses: 'While it serves no one's interests, particularly the proprietor, to continue supporting a business beyond the point of no return, the banking industry is very much committed to maintaining and extending its support to the vast majority of businesses which are capable of weathering the storm.'

One might expect the banks to make more use of the Loan Guarantee Scheme. In the past year the number of loans has increased but many amount to less than £15,000 and can therefore be processed by the banks with the minimum formality. Barclays constantly reminds its managers to make use of the scheme. NatWest reports increased use of the LGS, but Lloyds reports a fall off.

The Loan Guarantee Scheme provides loans of up to £100,000, repayable over a period of between three and seven years. The Government guarantees 70 per cent of the principal sum and the borrower pays a premium equal to 1.75 per cent of the total loan. Use of the LGS is relevant for businesses which could not obtain loans under normal bank requirements – usually because they have no track record or cannot provide security – but, it must be stressed, this is not a means of funding 'no hope' businesses.

Increasingly, the banks recognise the need to provide customers with the services they require rather than the services the bank believes they should receive. Alan Vaughan, Barclays' business sector marketing director, sets out the priorities under three headings:

- People: the quality of the bank's main contact with a small business, the continuity of that contact and the quality of support staff.

- Expertise: knowledge of a business – and therefore its needs.

- Quality of service: speed of the bank's decision-making, undertaking and implementation of instructions. Basically the bank should deliver what the customer wants at a competitive price.

The level of customer satisfaction is greater than it was a year ago. Some improvement can be attributed to the fact that the Big Four banks have invested considerable funds to improve their managers' understanding of business and corporate customers' needs.

Banks recognise the need, in current trading conditions, to form positive relationships with customers to ensure that they are aware of the situation before any problem gets out of hand. Cracknell asserts: 'Then we stand a fair chance of being able to help. The reverse is true when we are faced with effectively a *fait accompli* at the eleventh hour.'

Lloyds now monitors its small-business customers' cash flow more carefully and works closer with them. Garland declares: 'The essence of any good business relationship is communication and nowhere is this more pertinent than banking, especially now.'

According to White: 'Hard times inevitably mean that we get closer to our business customers. In an ideal world we would like that close working relationship on an ongoing basis.'

Hunter takes the same line: 'Wise customers talk to their bank managers. Bad times offer us an opportunity to get near to those who need nursing.'

Hunter has some advice for the owner-manager:

- Review your financial projections and if you identify a potential problem talk to your bank manager. He is more likely to be supportive if you can forecast a cash-flow hiccup rather than if he has to inform you that your overdraft limit has been breached.

- Use your bank to obtain credit references for new clients before extending credit terms. Many businesses experience difficulties as a result of bad debts which could have been avoided.

All the banks offer schemes to assist small businesses,

particularly start-ups. An imaginative idea from Lloyds is to provide businesses which have been established for less than two years with a year's free subscription to Dun & Bradstreet's Commercial Collection Service.

As I have already said, some small businesses perceive bank managers as business assassinators, headmasters or, at best, spoilsports. Hardly an ideal perspective. Remember: communication is a two-way business. If you foresee difficulties in keeping to your cash-flow forecast or problems in terms of a trading downturn or bad debts talk to your bank manager. Today.

MAKING THE BEST OF A BAD DEBT

The receipt of a letter headed: 'In the matter of the Insolvency Act 1986 – Notice to creditors', or 'Notice of creditors' meeting', may be the first intimation a business-man has that a customer is in financial trouble. This will come as a particularly unwelcome surprise if his business is owed a substantial sum of money. The initial reaction is usually one of frustration, closely followed by uncertainty as to what action can be taken to recover funds or, at least, salvage something. Appropriate action depends on the type of insolvency:

Administrative receivership

An administrative receiver must notify creditors of his appointment within 28 days, and convene a creditors' meeting within three months.

An administrative receiver is called in by a secured creditor whose security is in jeopardy. His duty is to distribute funds to the holder of a fixed charge. But before he can distribute funds under a floating charge, he must pay preferential debts in full. The receiver is not empowered to distribute funds to unsecured creditors. Unsecured creditors are, however, given the opportunity to study the receiver's report. This will detail events leading up to the receiver's appointment, make proposals for the distribution of assets and contain a breakdown of the funds owed to various classes of creditors.

Any creditor may attend the meeting of creditors, and may seek to be elected to the Creditors' Committee which is provided with information by the receiver.

Administrative receivership may precede liquidation or a voluntary arrangement.

Creditors' voluntary liquidation

In this event, notice of the creditors' meeting is issued on behalf of the board of directors. This must be held within 14 days of the shareholders' meeting which approved the resolution for a creditors' voluntary liquidation. Such a liquidation is triggered when the directors become aware that the company is insolvent and cannot continue trading. An unsecured creditor will not be paid the amount owed in full, or on time. A claim and a proxy form should be submitted.

Compulsory liquidation

The first notification of a compulsory liquidation is likely to be issued by the Official Receiver. The Official Receiver is a government official who is appointed by the Court to act as liquidator following the petition of a creditor whose debt exceeds £750. He may call a creditors' meeting in order to arrange for a licensed insolvency practitioner – usually a chartered accountant – to replace him and appoint a liquidation committee.

For a creditor, the implications of such a liquidation commence when a petition for a winding-up order is made. After that time, it is unlikely that creditors will receive payments in respect of any debts due, and it may be that amounts received subsequently will have to be repaid. Claim and proxy forms should be submitted to the Official Receiver before the meeting.

Administration

Administrations were introduced by the Insolvency Act 1986. The purpose of an administration is to provide an alternative to liquidation for an insolvent company in the event that an administrative receiver cannot be appointed because no debenture holder is willing to make the appointment.

It may be that an administration results in the company's survival, a voluntary arrangement or compromise with creditors, or liquidation. It is essential for creditors to attend, or be represented, at the creditors' meeting which must be called within three months of the administrator's appoint-ment. Questions will be asked and proposals made which should be considered, approved or amended. A creditor's chances of recovering a debt may depend on the part he plays at the meeting.

Administration is particularly harsh on creditors with rights over specific assets. Without leave of the Court, suppliers with retention of title clauses may not recover their goods; nor may leasing or hire-purchase companies repossess their property.

Voluntary arrangements

A voluntary arrangement will be proposed either during an administration, or when a company proposes an arrangement to discharge its debts to creditors by delayed or part payment. This is likely to happen if there is a possibility of the business surviving. Creditors may recoup more of their funds than they would from a liquidation, either because their debtor is rescued or an orderly rundown of the debtor's business produces a better return than immediate closure.

A company usually applies to the Court for a voluntary arrangement and nominates an insolvency practitioner to act as supervisor of the arrangement. A notice to creditors and details of the proposals are issued by the supervisor. Creditors should attend the meeting, or be represented, in order to influence decisions.

Bankruptcy

Bankruptcy only applies to individuals with debts of at least £750. A petition for a bankruptcy order can be presented to the Court after a statutory demand or unsatisfied execution of a judgement. If an order is made, the Official Receiver will be notified and a creditors' meeting called. In the majority of cases, the Official Receiver will have closed the bankrupt's business down and taken steps to realise any assets. As before, claim and proxy forms should be submitted to the Official Receiver.

Creditors' meetings, proxies and proofs of debt

The notice of a creditors' meeting must specify the place, date and time it will be held. It should also give the date and time by which a proxy must be lodged. Limited companies must nominate a proxy if a representative is to attend the creditors' meeting. The notice invariably asks for a statement of account or proof of debt to be lodged with the company or the insolvency practitioner.

While a limited company cannot attend a creditors' meeting, an officer of the company can appoint a person – a member of staff or professional adviser – to attend by use of the proxy form. A partnership must follow the same procedure if it is to be represented. A sole trader or individual creditor can attend in his own right, but may prefer a representative to attend, in which case a proxy form should be completed.

Appointment of a proxy is particularly important in liquidations and bankruptcies, in that a vote at the creditors' meeting decides which insolvency practitioner is to be the liquidator or administer the insolvent estate. The selection is made by counting the votes in terms of monetary value.

Completion of the proxy forms and proof of debt does not pose a problem. Professional advisers, such as accountants, offer such assistance and can act as representatives at creditors' meetings.

It is not advisable to appoint the company's chairman as proxy. This merely serves to put the creditor's vote in the hands of the self-same company which has just lost creditors' funds. A representative can question directors independently on the creditor's behalf and many accountancy firms offer this as a free service.

Prevention is the best cure

Unfortunately, action taken after receiving notice of a creditors' meeting is much like shutting the proverbial stable door. The earlier a creditor suspects that a customer may be suffering financial strain, the greater the chance of limiting losses – a subject addressed in the following chapter.

Appointment of a liquidator

If liquidation proceedings have commenced, a creditor, having failed to obtain payment or return of goods supplied, may wish to propose an insolvency practitioner he knows and trusts to act as liquidator, possibly his own accountant. A valid proxy form must be submitted and it is important that the creditor, or his representative, attends the creditors' meeting to support the proposal for the appointment of his nominee.

Administrative receivers and liquidators, administrators and the Official Receiver are all required to call meetings and provide reports. There is little individual creditors can do to speed up the processes of administration and liquidation. It usually becomes apparent, soon after the appointment, how much creditors can expect to receive, and further legal proceedings are unlikely to add substantially to the amount recovered.

Should you receive a 'Notice to creditors', do not ignore it. Complete the forms, attend the meetings and obtain what benefits you can by enforcing your rights.

How to Avoid Bad Debts

Many businesses are finding it difficult to maintain turnover, let alone increase it, under the current economic conditions and, in all too many instances, cash-flow budgets are not being met. It follows, therefore, that many businesses are simply not paying their debts as they become due.

Against such a background it is essential for owner-managers to consider what steps can be taken to reduce exposure to insolvent customers and unpaid debts.

Credit control

Sales are usually transacted on credit terms, with payment generally falling due during the course of the following month. A business intent on avoiding bad debts should carefully monitor its sales-ledger accounts to ensure that customers pay on time. A regular system of reviewing debts should be introduced and procedures established for chasing debtors for payment. Remember: a telephone call or fax message can prove more effective than a routine account rendered or stereotyped letter.

The next stage may be to instruct your solicitor or debt-collecting agent to write a letter. It is surprising how the intimation of possible legal proceedings can elevate your unpaid account to the top of the pile.

The trick is to maintain contact with the debtor. Remember: those who exert the greatest pressure will, in all probability, be paid first.

Take care with new customers. Obtain references and, if doubtful, ask to see the company's accounts. Do not allow too much credit during the early stages.

A supplier who suspects that a customer may not adhere to normal credit terms could ask for payment to coincide with the delivery of goods. It could issue a pro-forma invoice and require payment before the goods are delivered.

If an account is overdue, it is important to ascertain precisely why payment has not been received. It could be that some fault has been found in the goods or services. The invoice may be incorrect. Perhaps a credit is due.

On the other hand, the customer may be experiencing cash-flow problems, in which case you might be able to accommodate him by agreeing a slightly extended period for payment.

If a substantial sum is involved, it may be worth authorising a detailed investigation of the customer's affairs. This is usually carried out by the creditor's accountant.

My colleague, Christopher Morris, favours such inquiries. In his words: 'They often prove beneficial to both parties because they can lead to a reorganisation of the debtor company and improved prospects of recovery for the client.' Your accountant must be informed of the situation as early as possible – before the debtor's situation becomes chronic.

Loss limitation

If, after carrying out such informal procedures, the supplier has received no satisfaction, he must opt for stronger action.

He may decide to issue a statutory demand to the debtor. If the debtor does not comply with this within 21 days, the supplier can commence liquidation or bankruptcy proceedings. A winding-up petition has to be advertised in the press and this is bound to damage the debtor's business.

The debtor's bank manager will, in all probability, close the account as soon as he learns of the winding-up petition. This, of course, makes it most unlikely that the supplier will be paid without going through some form of insolvency process.

Another course open to the supplier is to commence recovery proceedings through the issue of a writ. A solicitor's advice will be needed as to procedure and to which court the application should be made. A judgment will be obtained which will include an order of the court for payment of a specific sum of money.

If a creditor is unable to obtain payment from a debtor whom he believes has sufficient tangible assets to pay the debt, a writ of execution can be obtained from the court. This is a court order to the sheriff or bailiffs to seize and release the debtor's assets – not a liquidation situation. It is usually best for a creditor to take action to recover a debt before a liquidator or administrator is appointed. If the judgment is not satisfied, liquidation or bankruptcy proceedings can follow.

For debts of less than £500 a creditor should consider pursuing the debtor through the small claims' procedure in the county court. However, as with all legal proceedings, bear in mind that there is little point in winning an action if the defendant does not have the money to pay the judgment debt.

Recovery of goods

Many suppliers incorporate a clause which has the effect of retaining title to the goods until they are paid for. If drafted effectively and brought to the customer's attention at the time of the order, the supplier may have a right to recover goods subject to identification.

When dealing with liquidators and administrative receivers in these circumstances, specific identification becomes most important. The only way to ensure identification is to use serial numbers or attach batch or order numbers – which can be specifically related to invoices – to the goods. Unfortunately, this is not always practical.

As soon as a supplier becomes aware of a customer's insolvency he should inspect the stocks to identify his goods and establish the quantity held by the customer.

The supplier may decide to remove his goods – providing it is with the customer's consent. Alternatively, he may wish to register his instructions in writing in relation to those goods: for example, not to be used or sold but held to the supplier's order pending agreement of the legal position.

Lien

The Insolvency Act 1986 has reduced the value of liens as far as creditors are concerned.

Creditors who hold goods belonging to an insolvent company on which they have incurred costs may, in certain circumstances, be able to retain those goods as a means to obtain payment.

Liens are complicated and expert advice should always be sought.

Set-offs

The same is true of set-offs, which are limited in application to those situations where debts and credits arise within the same legal entities.

Insolvency processes

If a creditor is unable to obtain recovery or reach agreement with a debtor, it may be necessary to precipitate formal insolvency. This is a last resort and professional advice should be taken before reaching a decision. But, if other methods have failed and the debtor company's position is deteriorating under existing management, it may be the only solution.

Insolvency procedures can be initiated in several ways:

- By issuing a petition for the compulsory winding up of the company. This is terminal and would be the appropriate course only when you have given up all hope of receiving full payment and have ceased to do business with the debtor.

- By appointing an administrative receiver. This is the course of action you could take where you have a charge over certain of the debtor's assets to secure amounts owing to you. The appointment of an administrative receiver allows the business to continue trading and gives an opportunity for reorganisation, at the same time as enabling your debt to be settled.

- By serving a petition for the appointment of an administrator. This could be appropriate where you do not have a charge over the debtor's assets.

  During the period of the administration the debtor would be protected and there would be an opportunity for reorganisation which could lead to a voluntary arrangement on the one hand or liquidation on the other. Even if the business does not continue, the administrator may be able to ensure a better and more ordered realisation of the debtor's assets than would be the case in a liquidation.

- By encouraging a customer to enter into a voluntary arrangement. This would be appropriate where temporary problems exist and would usually come about only after an administrator had been appointed.

  The voluntary arrangement might take the form of a compromise, a composition of debts or a moratorium, during which time the business would continue under close supervision.

Action

The name of the game is to limit risk and exposure. The following courses of action should be taken as quickly as possible:

- Review your system of credit control.

- Keep debtors under constant review and chase them continuously.

- Consider the various ways of obtaining payment as soon as a debt becomes overdue.

- Consider authorising an investigation of the debtor company's financial affairs if the sum is large and the customer is important to your business.

- Consider whether you should precipitate the insolvency of a debtor.

- Take professional advice early rather than late.

DIRECTORS IN DANGER

My neighbour David appears to be in some difficulty. David's problems began four or five years ago when, in search of a new challenge, he was invited to become a director of a local property development company. David was rather flattered and accepted with alacrity.

Some two years later, David confided that the directorship did not take up much time; meetings were held quarterly and there was little paperwork. The most significant aspect of the board meetings appeared to be the gourmet lunch which followed.

More recently, David told me that some of the company's developments seemed to be somewhat highly geared and he was concerned as to whether they could be sold at budgeted prices.

Now we learn that David's company has gone into liquidation and he has been warned that he is in danger of being declared an unfit person to be a director of a company. Worse, he may be liable to contribute to the assets of the company because the firm continued to trade after it became insolvent. Finally, it appears that David might also have to pay substantial fines in respect of the company's failure to keep proper records or file returns with Companies House.

David admits: 'I didn't know what was going on. I just went along with the other directors. I didn't think I was doing anything wrong.'

Unfortunately, David is not alone. Many people think that a directorship is an honour and privilege and are only too happy to receive a director's fee, however small, without realising their duties and responsibilities or what risks are attached to the position.

Since the Insolvency Act 1986 and the Company Director's Disqualification Act 1986 came into force, the likelihood of a company director being disqualified and made personally liable for the company's debts has increased.

An insolvency practitioner – usually a liquidator or receiver – now has a statutory duty to report on the conduct of directors and shadow directors of failed companies. If the practitioner uncovers evidence of activities which he believes could lead a court to declare that a director is unfit, he must make a report to the Department of Trade and Industry.

The DTI can then apply for a court order on the grounds of the person's unfitness to serve as a director. The maximum period of disqualification that can be imposed by a court is 15 years. While disqualified, a person may not be a director of any company or take any part in its management.

When deciding whether to disqualify a director, the court takes into account several factors in terms of directors' responsibilities:

- Breach of faith or duty owed by a director to a company.

- The use of company assets for a director's own benefit.

- The removal of company assets beyond the reach of directors.

- The company's failure to keep proper records or file statutory returns.

- Failure to produce annual accounts.

- Causing a company's insolvency.

- Failure to supply customers who have prepaid, or make repayment of deposits.

- Transactions by the company which are liable to be set aside under insolvency law.

- Failures in connection with calling the meeting of a creditors' voluntary liquidation.

- Failure in an insolvency to comply with duties relating to statements of affairs, attendance at meetings, surrender of company property and co-operation with insolvency office holders.

Such duties and responsibilities also extend to shadow directors – legally defined as: 'A person in accordance with whose directions or instructions the directors of the company are accustomed to act.'

The disqualification of shadow directors is intended to catch those who run companies through 'front men'. The term 'shadow director' may include outside persons or corporate bodies who, often for legitimate commercial reasons, influence the directors' actions. Included in this category are bankers who, in exercising 'intensive care' of a company with problems, should take care that they are not in danger of being classed as shadow directors.

The 1986 insolvency legislation heightens the possibility of directors being held personally liable for a company's debts. In certain circumstances, a director can be held personally liable to company creditors. However, most of the personal liability provisions apply only when the company is in liquidation, and involve the director contributing to the company assets for distribution by the liquidator.

Directors must also be wary of 'wrongful trading'. This is not a question of fraudulent action, which is a criminal offence and includes people other than directors or shadow directors. Current legislation requires a director to recognise when his company cannot avoid insolvent liquidation. This is when the company's assets cannot be realised for a sum sufficient to pay all creditors and costs of liquidation in full.

It is then a director's duty to take immediate action to protect creditors' interests. If he does not take such action, he runs the risk of 'wrongful trading' and the court may order him to make a contribution to the company's assets.

To obtain such an order the procedure is similar to obtaining a disqualification order. If the court makes an order against a director for wrongful trading, it may also make a disqualification order, without a separate application.

When a court considers a director's conduct, it will not only take into account the director's activities, but will assume that he possesses the competence and expertise expected of a director fulfilling his role in the organisation. The court is unlikely to look favourably on excuses such as the director was not kept informed or did not know the true position.

Whether a company is insolvent is inevitably a finance-related question. Any director with financial qualifications or with responsibility for accounting – even if he does not perform the function himself but relies on book-keeping staff – is more likely to be found liable for wrongful trading. A high degree of responsibility is expected of a managing director in view of his key role.

A non-executive director's position depends on his precise role, but he cannot expect to avoid responsibility simply because he is not involved in day-to-day business management. The non-executive's monitoring role is assumed to be one of significant responsibility.

In order to minimise the risk of being found liable for wrongful trading, a director should:

- Ensure that his job description is accurately defined. In particular, his role should not include anything of which he is not capable.

- Ensure that the company has a system for producing management accounts and information on time – in a form which details the company's present financial position, trading and cash-flow projections.

If a director believes insolvent liquidation is inevitable and he cannot persuade his colleagues of the seriousness of the situation, he is in a difficult position. At this stage he should insist on having his concern recorded in the board minutes. This serves to make the position of other directors, in the event of an insolvency, that much more awkward, because they will be unable to plead ignorance of the situation. If such dissent is not recorded, the director should deliver a letter to the company secretary and take legal advice on his position. Resignation in the absence of such a recording will not necessarily absolve the director of his duties to the creditors.

Let there be no misunderstanding: directorships should not be undertaken lightly. At a time when many companies are experiencing problems with profits and cash flow, directors would be well advised to review their position and make sure they are fully up to date with the facts and figures.

As David now realises, it is no fun to be described as an unfit person to hold a directorship.

SELF-PRESERVATION

EMPLOYED OR SELF-EMPLOYED?

Many people are in business 'on their own account' as 'freelances' or 'consultants'. This can mean that they are self-employed; on the other hand, it can mean that they are employed. But, when it comes to such matters as income tax, national insurance, the treatment of expenses and pension arrangements, there are significant differences.

If you start your own business – selling goods or supplying services to a wide range of customers – or go into partnership with others, it is obvious that you are self-employed.

Equally, if you are a full-time employee of a company, with an appropriate contract, it is obvious that you are employed.

However, there are many instances where it is not clear and, by taking appropriate action, you may be able to influence your status. Computer buffs, financial consultants, lorry drivers and gardeners, take note.

Then again, you may have taken early retirement and chosen to work part-time for your previous employer, while carrying out work for other businesses.

Generally speaking, it is attractive to be treated as self-employed because:

- The income or profit derived from your business will be subject to income tax on a 'previous-year' basis – sometime after you have received it – whereas income from employment is subject to tax at the time of payment under PAYE arrangements.

- Expenses can be deducted from self-employed earnings, providing they are 'wholly and exclusively' incurred for business purposes. The expenses you may claim as an employed person must meet the additional test of being 'necessarily' incurred in the performance of the duties of your employment – an altogether more stringent and difficult test.

● The self-employed pay flat-rate national insurance of £5.15 per week, plus a profit-related contribution (up to a maximum of £906 per annum). In the case of employed persons, both employer and employee contribute. On income up to £20,280, the combined rate is 19.4 per cent.

On the other hand, those who are self-employed must register for VAT if their supply of goods or services exceeds £35,000 in the financial year. What must also be considered are the administration costs involved in being self-employed: the need to keep records of income and expenditure, along with business expenses such as travel, telephone, typing, stationery, etc.

Anyone in this borderline area between employed and self-employed will need to satisfy the Inland Revenue and the Department of Social Security before they are accepted as self-employed. Until this is agreed, they are likely to be dealt with as employed persons and those for whom they work will be required to deal with them as employees, deducting PAYE and national insurance accordingly.

In order to determine status, the basic test applied by the authorities is to ask whether someone performing services or supplying goods is doing so as the representative of a separate business which is under his control? Or, put another way, is there a contract of service (which means employment) or a contract for services (which means self-employment)?

There is no simple answer to this question, but there are a number of indicators as to how the Inland Revenue and DSS are likely to respond. The existence of a separate business to provide services is not conclusive. It may still be the case that the person is involved in what actually amounts to a contract of service.

It is necessary to go deeper:

● Is there a written contract or correspondence to demonstrate a contract for services? Can it be shown that the contract has been followed (intention is not the key, facts are)?

● Does the person control the arrangements? Does he decide how goods or services will be provided, in what way, when, and where? What is important is the right of control.

● Does the person operate from his own premises? If he works at his customer's premises, is it clear that he is not subject to staff regulations, does not work set hours and does not take set periods of holiday?

● Is it clear that he can use deputies to perform the work or does he have to perform it himself? Is it clear that he may provide, and hold himself out as being able to provide, services to several parties at the same time?

● If equipment is required, is this provided by the person and is the upkeep his responsibility?

● Does the person take the financial risk if, for example, the project makes a loss? Does he provide capital? Does he pay insurance premiums in respect of public liability and professional indemnity, if appropriate?

● Is it clear that payments received are calculated by reference to the goods and services provided? Are invoices issued? Is the person registered for VAT?

● Is it clear that services can be provided to other parties according to choice and is work carried out for others? Evidence of a range of customers strengthens the argument.

● Is it clear that the customer can terminate the arrangements in accordance with any agreed terms and is not subject to any statutory requirements as to notice of dismissal?

The Inland Revenue and the DSS will liase to ensure that treatment in relation to both taxes is uniform. Local tax offices have the authority to make a ruling for both. If doubt over status exists, an opinion can be sought in advance from the authorities. Case presentation is important and advice should be taken from an accountant.

There are persons who, by virtue of express statutory provisions or decisions by the authorities may, in appropriate circumstances, be treated as employees.

These include certain ministers of religion, lecturers, teachers engaged by educational establishments, persons supplied by or through agencies, rent officers, au pairs and office cleaners.

Persons regarded as self-employed include foster parents, home workers and out workers, subcontractors who hold tax-exemption certificates, umpires, tennis coaches and volunteer development workers engaged abroad.

More recently, the Revenue has made concerted and successful attempts to redesignate certain categories of work as employed rather than self-employed. For example, actors and actresses with 'standard' Equity contracts are now generally regarded as employed. Doctors have come under attack, in that income they receive from various part-time appointments should be dealt with under PAYE and not included in self-employment profits.

In a recent case, the Court of Appeal held that casual wine waiters were employees. In another case, the House of Lords held that a pastor of the Presbyterian Church of Wales did not have a contract of service and was therefore self-employed.

It is the facts of the case which will decide whether a person is employed or self-employed. What must be ensured is that the arrangements made amount to a contract for services and there is evidence to support the case.

REMUNERATION OR DIVIDEND?

Most entrepreneurs need to take money out of their business – if only to meet everyday living costs – and the manner in which this is done is dictated by the structure of the business.

At the time of starting up a business the owner usually has the choice of operating as a sole proprietor or partnership (possibly with husband/wife) or as a limited company.

In making this choice, he will bear in mind the following facts:

- Operating as a sole proprietor or partnership is simpler in that there is no need for formal documents (although some form of written partnership agreement is desirable).

- The procedure of starting up is simpler, free of many of the formalities of companies and therefore cheaper.

- National insurance rates for the self-employed are lower than for employed people.

- If you suffer losses, you will be able to set them off against your other income for tax purposes and, if you make losses early on, you will be able to set them against income from the three previous years – even before you started in business.

The main argument in favour of starting up as a limited company is the limitation of liability for the shareholder. Unless you give personal guarantees to the company's bankers, your liability for the company's debts will be limited to the amount you have subscribed by way of share capital. The rate of corporation tax for a small company (pre-tax profits of up to £250,000) is only 25 per cent which gives you an opportunity to retain profits for expansion of the business. You may find it easier to obtain finance for a company, as banks and investors prefer to invest in a corporate structure rather than in a partnership or an individual. Since the ownership of a company can be divided up into shares, family members and other third parties can participate in the business without becoming employees.

There is a compromise between personal ownership and a limited liability company: the business can start as a sole proprietorship or partnership and, when it is established and making a reasonable profit, can convert into a company. If planned with care, the business can often be transferred into a new company without any additional tax liabilities.

In a partnership, income tax and national insurance are based on the profits, as shown in the accounts, which are calculated without making a deduction in respect of partners' remuneration. It therefore makes no difference when the proprietors draw out funds required for living expenses, etc. Assuming that money is available in the business, it should be withdrawn at a time convenient to both the business and the proprietor. As a matter of practice, partners will often draw a minimum amount on account through the financial year and draw the balance when the results are known.

In such circumstances, there is no particular advantage in leaving undrawn profits in the business which will, in any event, attract income tax at the partners' top rates and, likewise, national insurance.

In the case of a company, the choices are more complicated. As already mentioned the corporation tax rate for small companies is only 25 per cent on profits up to £250,000, while a sliding scale means that the new standard 33 per cent rate is not charged until profits reach £1 million or more. There can, therefore, be an advantage in terms of tax and cash flow in leaving profits in the company. This will certainly be the case if the proprietors already earn sufficient income from the company or elsewhere to take them into the higher-rate tax band.

Indeed, one of the objectives of the small companies' rate is to encourage profit retention so that firms can fund expansion and increase their working capital. On the other hand, the owner/manager should be alive to the fact that the retention of profits in a company will serve to increase the net asset value which could result in a higher liability to capital gains tax in the event of a sale of shares.

If one follows this argument through, there is a case for proprietors drawing out all the profits, particularly in view of the fact that the top rate of personal income tax and capital gains tax may not always be as low as 40 per cent. But this ignores the most important element of the equation, namely that the retention of profits is the most effective way of funding a company's expansion, not only because the funds are in the business, but also because such profits will provide a foundation for obtaining additional bank loans.

The next point to consider is how to draw profits out of a limited company. Should it be in the form of remuneration or dividend? At one time, earned income suffered less tax than unearned, so the owner-manager was encouraged to take his share of the company's profits as salary or bonus. It has always been possible, and indeed usual, to provide the owner-manager with part of his emoluments in the form of benefits' such as a company car or the provision of a cheap loan.

What we are concerned with is whether the cash element should be in the form of salary and bonus or dividend. This assumed new importance in the 1990/91 tax year as a result of the separate income-tax treatment of husband and wife. Clearly there are tax advantages in providing both husband and wife with sufficient income to absorb personal allowances and, ideally, the basic-rate band as well. But remuneration, to be allowable for tax purposes, must be reasonable and a proper reflection of the services performed. Employing one's wife as a part-time secretary is unlikely to warrant anything like £20,000 per annum.

Remuneration and dividends possess advantages and disadvantages:

- Remuneration is subject to PAYE income tax and national insurance at the time of payment. The top rates of national insurance are 10.4 per cent for the employer and nine per cent for the employee. As far as the employee is concerned, his contributions are capped when remuneration reaches £390 per week (1991/92), but the employer pays 10.4 per cent however high the remuneration. As the Inland Revenue require PAYE and national insurance to be paid by the 19th of the tax month following payment, there is little scope for credit.

- Remuneration forms the basis of the pension entitlement of the owner-manager. As a general guide, a pension from an approved scheme cannot exceed two-thirds of your remuneration with, in certain circumstances, a cap on the amount of remuneration. This was £60,000 for 1989/90 and, with annual indexation, has risen to £71,400 for 1991/92. Clearly, if the employer pays the owner-manager a salary of only £5000, and distributes everything else by way of dividend, there will only be a small pension entitlement.

- Dividends are paid to shareholders, irrespective of whether they are directors or number among those who work and contribute to the company's success. This offers business owners the flexibility to issue or transfer shares to a spouse so that he/she will have an opportunity of receiving income without the restrictions which apply to payment of a salary or bonus. On the other hand, it can breed resentment between 'workers' and 'owners'.

- A dividend is treated as income of the recipient when it is paid.

The company will be required to pay advance corporation tax (ACT) equal to one-third of the dividend payment at the end of the quarter in which the dividend is paid. The ACT will be allowed as a deduction from the mainstream corporation-tax liability for the period in which the dividend is payable – assuming that the company has earned profits for corporation-tax purposes. Mainstream corporation tax is payable nine months after the end of the financial period. Any unused ACT can be carried back for up to six years or forward for relief in later years.

The individual will be treated as having paid basic-rate tax on the grossed-up amount of the dividend payment. He may be liable to higher-rate tax, depending on the amount of his total income in that tax year. If so the higher rate tax will be payable on 1 December following the end of the tax year. The following conclusions may be drawn from this:

- There is a case for drawing out all a company's profits unless they are needed for the maintenance and development of the business. Even then, it is quite possible for the director or shareholder to draw profits out and return them as a loan, with or without interest.

- Some part of the profits should be drawn as remuneration to provide an adequate base for pension contributions. This is an area which requires specialist advice. It is not important when remuneration is drawn unless there are indications that income-tax rates or national insurance are likely to change.

- Amounts not required as remuneration should be taken out in the form of dividends. From the individual's point of view, it is probably beneficial to receive dividends early in the tax year so that there is a maximum interval before payment of any higher-rate income tax which may be due from the shareholder.

  From the point of view of the company, it is likely to be beneficial to pay the dividend just before the end of the financial year, rather than just after, so the reduction in mainstream corporation-tax liability can be obtained as early as possible.

  There is a small benefit to be had from paying dividends early in the quarter rather than late, in order to obtain longer credit on the amount of ACT due to be paid. By way of example, a company with a December year-end might pay a dividend in mid-October and one with a June year-end in mid-April.

- You should consider whether the ownership of a company gives you the opportunity to provide your spouse with income in order to make use of both sets of personal allowances (£3295 each plus the £1720 married couple's allowance for the husband), and the basic-rate band (£23,700). If a wife is paying half the mortgage interest as well as some charitable covenants, she could receive an income in the region of £29,000 before she pays higher-rate income tax.

Separate Taxation

Husbands and wives will be aware that, since 6 April 1990, their tax affairs have been dealt with separately. The changes which independent taxation brought in are intended to remedy a long-standing complaint that traditional rules for taxing married couples involved an invasion of married women's privacy in their financial affairs.

The alterations were not intended to offer new tax planning opportunities and the average married couple will have discovered that they are not materially affected by the changeover.

For 1990/91 and future years, everyone is taxed on his or her own income (including investment income) after deducting a single personal allowance (£3005 for 1990/91 and £3295 for 1991/92). The husband has not lost any allowances: instead of receiving a married man's allowance, as before, he now receives a single personal allowance and, in addition, a new married couple's allowance (£1720 for 1990/91 and 1991/92). This allowance is index-linked in the same way as other personal allowances.

The wife receives a full single personal allowance in her own right. This is available for use against any income, not just against earned income. The husband can surrender to his wife any amount of the married couple's allowance which, due to a lack of income, he is unable to use himself.

It is immediately apparent that, where the wife previously received sufficient earnings to obtain a full earned income allowance and the couple's combined income was subject to basic-rate tax, the allowances which they now receive, and hence the tax paid, will not be materially different.

Generally speaking, those who save in terms of tax will be those who would have previously benefited from an election for separate taxation of the wife's earnings. Such couples are now able to claim the married couple's allowance as well as two single personal allowances.

Also, where the wife's earned income is negligible but significant unearned income is enjoyed, she is now able to claim a personal allowance instead of a restricted earned-income allowance.

Separate taxation means extra time and extra expense. Husband and wife each have to submit tax returns for the year ended 5 April 1991 and subsequent years. There are separate tax assessments and separate payments of tax liabilities.

Should husband and wife use accountants or other professional advisers to deal with their tax affairs, separate letters of engagement are required for husband and wife and separate bills for services provided.

Husband and wife must consider whether they wish to keep their affairs confidential or whether each is prepared to let the other know details of their taxation and financial circumstances.

The accountant's job is made simpler if there is no requirement for confidentiality because he does not have to deal with husband and wife as two separate and unconnected clients – a factor which should keep the increase in fees within bounds.

Although the switch to separate taxation was not intended to provide tax planning opportunities, some do exist.

Clearly, the planning opportunities revolve around making sure that both spouses use their allowances, both single persons and married couples, and their basic-rate tax bands, so that the amount of combined income which attracts tax at 40 per cent is kept to the minimum. In most families, this will involve a husband transferring income to his wife, since it is more common for a husband's income to exceed his wife's.

In the most extreme case, where a man is able to transfer income taxable at 40 per cent to his wife, who previously had no taxable income at all, the tax-saving for using the wife's personal allowance (£3295) and basic-rate band (£23,700) could amount to £4873 in 1991/92. The first essential must be that the husband receives an income of at least £5015 and the wife an income of at least £3295 to ensure that the personal allowances are used.

The couple must think and act as a team to take full advantage of the planning opportunities. Although this may come naturally to many couples, some will find it difficult to accept the inevitable loss of privacy and control over their finances.

In an age where divorce must be perceived as a high-risk event, many will be reluctant to transfer significant wealth to a spouse who just might disappear. It must also be said that one of the main reasons for implementing independent taxation was to improve and preserve privacy, not the opposite.

When considering a transfer of assets, the following should be borne in mind:

Income from jointly owned assets such as investments, bank accounts and property is attributable half to the husband and half to the wife. However, the couple may vary this by lodging with the Inspector of Taxes a declaration that their interests are split in some other ratio. This ratio must be the same as their respective interests in the asset.

Care should be taken to ensure that the assets transferred do not produce income when there is a restriction on repayment of income tax. In 1990/91, interest on most bank and building-society deposit accounts was subject to composite-rate tax which cannot be repaid to the taxpayer.

In 1991/92 composite-rate tax ceases, so this unattractive facet of investment in banks and building societies has passed.

Mortgage interest payable may be shared between husband and wife in any proportion they choose and notify to the Inland Revenue. This proportion can be varied by way of further notification to the Revenue.

Apart from the transfer of assets between spouses, there are other ways in which one spouse can generate income for the other.

For example, a self-employed husband may pay a salary to his wife for assistance in running the business. The major obstacle is that the Inland Revenue will require that the salary does not exceed a commercial level.

If a higher level of income is desired, consideration should be given to forming a partnership between husband and wife. Care, however, will be needed to ensure that the partnership is bona fide and cannot be set aside by the Inland Revenue. Where the husband is the owner of a limited company, it may be possible for his wife to become a director and receive a salary, although once again the salary must be commercially supportable.

Or the wife could receive an investment income through a share issue: a special class of shares could be created to carry a high rate of dividend but with no voting rights and no significant rights to assets in the event of a liquidation.

The old facility whereby trading losses were transferred between spouses will be lost under independent taxation, so care must be taken not to leave one spouse with too high an income in a year where the other suffers losses; this can prove a problem where one or both spouses is a name at Lloyd's.

Similar principles apply in terms of capital gains tax. The objective should be to maximise the use of both spouses' annual exemptions along with basic-rate bands which have not been fully utilised for relieving income tax.

It may, therefore, be beneficial for one spouse to transfer an asset to the other so that the recipient may realise the asset and use the annual exemption to reduce or eliminate a capital-gains-tax liability.

In this context, note that where assets are jointly held, each spouse will be assessed on a proportion of the gain on disposal – 50:50 unless notified otherwise. This may be a way of ensuring that both exemptions are fully used.

As already stressed, the maximum saving of income tax is £4873. If a maximum capital-gains-tax saving of £2200 (£5500 at 40 per cent) is added, the potential annual tax saving for a couple rises to £7073.

Wealthy couples may feel that such a saving is too small to justify the major asset transfers entailed and the non-tax risks involved.

On the other hand, many may feel that any saving, such as might be derived from merely using the personal allowance, is well worth having. At the least it will go towards paying the accountant's fees for dealing with two taxation cases rather than one.

PENSIONS FOR PROFESSIONALS

For some self-employed, pension policies will represent their largest asset: the investment will exceed the cost of their house. It is a salutary thought that many will, year by year, pay the maximum premiums which qualify for tax relief only to end up with pensions significantly less than their final earnings. These will include partners in professional and commercial firms, executives and consultants who are not included in company pension schemes, and individuals who 'do their own thing'.

A major shake-up of self-employed pension arrangements took place on 1 July 1988. The old-style Retirement Annuity Policies (RAPs) were replaced with Personal Pension Plans (PPPs), but with the proviso that those who had contributed to RAPs could continue to do so. The major differences between the schemes are:

- Both schemes allow part of the pension entitlement to be commuted for a tax-free lump sum. However, a PPP limits this to 25 per cent of the underlying fund, whereas the amount available under RAP is geared to the individual's age at the time he takes his pension. For somebody aged 65 approximately one-third of the fund's value could be taken as cash.

- PPPs permit the pension to be drawn from the age of 50 (compared with 60 for RAPs).

- The percentage of net relevant earnings available for tax relief is, on the whole, higher for PPPs than for RAPs.

- There is a ceiling or 'cap' on PPPs in terms of the net relevant earnings eligible for tax relief. The cap was £60,000 for 1989/90 which is indexed in line with the Retail Prices Index. It rose to £64,800 in 1990/91 and £71,400 in 1991/92.

The effects of the different percentage and of the cap are set out in the table. As with RAPs, PPP payments can include both pension payments and premiums for life cover under the pension rules (whereby 5 per cent of earnings may be used to purchase cover against death before retirement).

Age on first day of tax year	RAP limits %	PPP limits % (1991/92)		Income limit above which RAPs give higher output (1991/92)
35 or less	17.5	17 5	£12,495	£71,400
36–45	17.5	20	£14,280	£81,600
46–50	17.5	25	£17,850	£102,000
51–55	20	30	£21,420	£107,100
56–60	22.5	35	£24,990	£111,067
61 and over	27.5	40	£28,560	£103,855

For the vast majority the decision as to whether to invest in RAPs or PPPs will be clear cut. Those who did not contribute to self-employed pension arrangements before 1 July 1988 have no option but to invest in PPPs.

Those who earned less than the earnings cap are likely to find that the PPP allowance is greater. On the other hand, RAPs produce a larger lump sum when the contributor retires or takes his benefits at the age of 60 or later. The best solution may be to pay the maximum permitted in the form of RAPs and top up with PPPs. This provides a wider investment spread and benefits which flow from the age of 50 (instead of 60 with RAPs).

Those who earn more than the earnings cap, but less than the RAP income limit, can invest either in existing RAPs or new PPPs. Payments in respect of PPPs by such individuals should be on a single premium 'one-off basis' and, in order to avoid complications, the maximum RAP contribution should, whenever practicable, be paid first with the PPP facility used merely as a 'top up'.

Those who earned substantially more than the earnings cap of £71,400 in 1991/92 – and above the income limit shown in the last column of the table – should, if possible, invest in existing RAPs. This way, their premiums will not be limited by reference to the earnings cap – as would be the case for PPPs. Although existing RAPs may be policies with single or annual premiums of relatively small amounts, it should be possible for assurance companies to vary their terms in order to accept additional single premiums or larger annual premiums.

If someone wishes to contribute wholly or partly to a PPP, he must recognise the £71,400 earnings cap and maximum contribution levels. Over-contribution to RAPs will render some, if not all, of the PPPs unallowable for tax. Moreover, unallowable PPPs must be cancelled or refunded and, in view of the fact that PPP providers are empowered to make deductions to recover their costs, this could prove an exceedingly expensive mistake.

The earnings cap obviously has its greatest impact on those with large incomes. A 40 year old earning £200,000 was permitted to pay premiums of £35,000 (17.5 per cent of £200,000) if he started his pension arrangement in 1988/89, but only £14,280 (20 per cent of £71,400) if he started in 1991/92. Although the earnings cap is indexed, the prospective retirement pension will be a much smaller proportion of final earnings than hitherto, and may well encourage greater investment in Business Expansion Schemes, PEPs and other tax-effective investments.

In general, those with existing RAPs in well-performing company funds should continue with contributions. If a PPP is held to obtain investment spread or additional life cover, it is preferable for payments to be made on a 'one-off' basis, so that the premium is not ongoing.

THE DIRECTOR'S DILEMMA

It is easy to forget the importance of pension provision to directors of small businesses but the question of what provisions to make and how best to make them can represent a very real dilemma.

Specific pension provision for the director of a small business would normally be made to a Director's (Executives') Pension Scheme funded directly out of the company's pre-tax profits. Ian Woodroffe, director of independent pensions advisers Towry Law, points out that the board of a successful private company has four options with regard to their profits:

- Retain profits within the company. Result: pay corporation tax.

- Pay dividends to the directors as shareholders. Result: pay income tax.

- Vote bonuses to directors. Result: pay income tax and additional company national insurance contributions.

- Make pension contributions. Result: save tax but possibly lose the use of all or part of the contributions within the business.

It must be remembered that to obtain relief against corporation tax in the current company year, pension contributions must be made during the same trading period. In particularly profitable years, it is possible to make a special contribution to the Directors' Pension Scheme in order to cover previously unpensioned or underpensioned earnings.

A special contribution to a Directors' Pension Scheme is fully allowable against corporation tax in the year of payment, provided that it does not exceed the normal annual contribution paid to all company pension arrangements by the business, or £20,000 if greater.

An alternative to the Directors' Pension Scheme is a Personal Pension Plan where the individual can decide how much to contribute: special contributions can be made by the individual to pick up any shortfalls arising as a result of previous years' unpensioned earnings. These could be funded by extra remuneration or a bonus from the company.

The Inland Revenue does not directly impose a limit on the level of contributions to a Directors' Pension Scheme but instead restricts the level of benefits that can be taken at retirement. In contrast, the Inland Revenue control of Personal Pension Plans is through a limit on the level of contribution with no limit on the benefits that flow. The result is that there may be greater scope for maximising contribution by way of a Personal Pension Plan if the director is young, but through a Directors' Pension Scheme if he is older.

According to Towry Law's calculation, a man of 50 on a salary of £40,000 with no previous pension provision and retirement planned for age 60, could justify his company making a first-year contribution of up to £111,638 (15 per cent higher for a woman) with subsequent annual payments of 50 per cent of this amount, but dependent upon future salary levels and investment returns.

In the case of a Personal Pension Plan the maximum contribution would be £10,000 plus up to six back-years' under-provision calculated at 25 per cent of earnings for 1988/89 and 1989/90, and 17.5 per cent for the earlier years.

Both the Directors' Pension Scheme and the Personal Pension Plan usually operate on a money purchase basis – i.e. the benefits at retirement are dependent on both the size of the contribution and investment results. As already mentioned, the maximum benefits that may be derived from a new Directors' Pension Scheme are dictated by the Inland Revenue and are as follows:

- A member's retirement pension of up to two-thirds of 'final remuneration' (after at least 20 years' service).

- A widow's reversionary pension of up to two-thirds of the member's pension at the time of death.

- Part of the member's retirement pension may be exchanged for a tax-free capital sum of up to 1.5 times 'final remuneration' (after at least 20 years' service).

- Pension payments may rise in line with increases in the RPI.

- Normal retirement age is between 60 and 70 but early retirement (with reduced maximum benefits) is possible from age 50 (or earlier in the event of serious ill-health).

- 'Portability'. Within a Directors' Pension Scheme, an individual's funds may be separately identified and, subject to Inland Revenue consent, are wholly transferable to a scheme with another company, a Personal Pension Plan or for the purchase of a Buy-out Policy from an insurance company.

There is a ceiling on final remuneration which cannot exceed £64,800 for 1990/91 and £71,400 for 1991/92 – rising each year in line with increases in the RPI. This only applies to scheme members who joined after the introduction of the earnings cap.

It is all very well to talk about substantial pension contributions, but can directors afford to lock away large amounts of profit in pension funds? What about expansion, re-equipment and capital investment? Arranging directors' pensions as a small self-administered scheme (SSAS) could well be the solution. At present an SSAS offers exceptional flexibility and potential for the company to utilise the funds held in the Directors' Pension Scheme. Some more common examples are:

- A loan to the company for specific commercial purposes (e.g. purchase of capital equipment or property improvement of up to 50 per cent of the fund value).

- Purchase of commercial property, including that occupied or to be occupied by the company.

- Purchase of company shares (subject to Inland Revenue clearance) provided the aggregate investment, including loans, in the employer company does not exceed 50 per cent of the value of the fund.

- Director investment in quoted or unquoted shares or in discretionary managed funds.

- Cash and gilts.

It should be borne in mind that a pension fund invested in factory buildings and equipment may not produce as good a pension as an insurance company fund invested in blue-chip stock.

Woodroffe points to a frequently overlooked advantage of an SSAS, which is the ability to pay pensions from the fund for up to five years after retirement. When the annuity is finally purchased, the director is older and should obtain better value from the life assurance company, particularly if the purchase can be timed to coincide with a period of high rates of interest.

Meanwhile, investment flexibility is retained, substantial life cover is also maintained (free of inheritance tax) and, if required, company assets can be retained in the pension fund and eventually passed on for the benefit of the next generation.

An SSAS can be expensive to arrange and so it is only good value if the size of funds is, or soon will be, in excess of some £40,000. Directors' requirements change, as does legislation, so even if the wider investment advantages are not immediately required it could be worth considering setting up a Directors' Pension Scheme with an insurance company under a self-administered trust.

Other points worthy of consideration when reviewing a Directors' Scheme include the following:

- Is the director's spouse employed by the company? If so, this second source of income should be included in the scheme to obtain a second pension and lump sum. The spouse on retirement will be able to set personal allowances and the basic-rate tax band against the pension income.

- Are the PIID benefits being pensioned? The scale charge

on company cars has gone up by more than 350 per cent over five years. As these benefits are taxable they are also pensionable.

- Can the director afford to delay increasing contributions? If funding for a specific benefit at age 60 begins at age 50, it could cost more than twice as much as it might have cost had contributions begun at age 40. This figure assumes that contributions increase in line with salary.

- Does the director need all his bonus? A director could forego part of his annual bonus in order that the company may make an additional contribution to his pension However, bonuses are pensionable remuneration and therefore subject to NI contributions. So care will be needed to ensure the pension contribution is properly documented.

- Has inheritance tax been considered? Directors' schemes and PPPs can be written under trust leaving the distribution of benefits to the trustees' discretion. This permits the lump-sum, death-in-service benefits to be paid to children and other relatives without an inheritance-tax liability.

In summary, it is important to remember that company circumstances differ and directors have differing priorities. With pensions legislation becoming more complex and no sign of a slackening in the pace of legislative change, it is becoming increasingly vital to take independent professional advice. Getting it right can guarantee a happy and prosperous retirement; getting it wrong can cost the director and company dear.

ACTION MAN IN RETIREMENT

The retirement of the breadwinner, be it a he or she, marks a major milestone.

Employment and Social Security legislation still regards 65 as the retirement age for men and 60 for women, but increasingly businesses are moving towards a retirement age of 60 and in some cases 55.

Whereas retirement used to be seen as something akin to the end of the road, it is now perceived as more of a junction or fork in the route of business life.

Many take early retirement out of choice and, during the run up to retirement, you will invariably ask yourself: What am I going to do when I retire? Will I be happy doing nothing? Do I have sufficient pension and capital to ensure that my spouse and I will be comfortable for the rest of our lives?

You will also consider: Will it drive either of us (or both) insane if I am at home every day? Do I need some occupation to keep me happy and fulfilled? What is my pension position? Will I need to earn some money? Can I afford to defer drawing my state, self-employed or company pension for some years?

Your answers to such questions will lead you to consider a number of possibilities.

Complete retirement

This means no business interest and no involvement in voluntary, community or other unpaid work. Such a person will need to be financially secure, motivated by things other than business: for example, travel, art, scholarship or horse-racing.

Going to live abroad may be your goal, but do not rush into it. Many have repented at leisure a decision made in haste. Cheaper living costs and more sunshine are not the only things in life.

Voluntary interests

This is the likely choice for business people who are financially secure and want to pursue new interests without regard to monetary reward.

There are numerous opportunities, including charitable or social work and local council, church or political activities. The prison parole board or a school governing board may beckon. The prospect of emerging as a magistrate or an Inland Revenue commissioner may also appeal. REACH is an organisation which places retired people in unpaid positions with charities.

All can prove satisfying. What you can be assured of is that if you possess skills and qualifications you will be much in demand.

Business activity

Many will seek stimulation from an involvement in business and not a few will be eager to supplement their income in order to maintain the standard of living established before retirement. Such involvement can range from a non-executive directorship or part-time consultancy to total involvement in running your own business.

Directorships and consultancies

If you have been successful in business prior to retirement and are well qualified, you may be offered positions as a non-executive director or consultant.

Such opportunities usually occur with businesses in which you were involved before retirement which want to benefit from your skills and experience.

The first step is to approach your business contacts and friends – sometime before retirement – to see what might be on offer. You may be able to discover younger people with a business idea and ambition to succeed who need your skills as an accountant, surveyor or sales director, for example, to complete their management team. You may even take a stake in their business at an early stage of its development. But you must be a good judge of people and be satisfied that the business proposal is viable.

The Department of Employment employs retired businessmen and women as counsellors for the Small Firms' Service and the Department of Trade and Industry has similar requirements for its Enterprise Initiative programme.

Intex is an organisation which specialises in executive leasing and uses mainly senior executives who have opted for early retirement.

There are numerous executive-search firms which specialise in providing non-executive directors – these, too, will include senior executives who are coming up to retirement. Two organisations prominent in this field are the Institute of Directors and Pro Ned.

Current trends point to greater opportunities for older executives, including those who have retired.

Foremost is the demographic phenomenon whereby the lower birth rates of the 1970s will result in a deepening shortage of skilled young people in the 1990s and beyond. To compensate we are likely to see more flexible age limits in executive appointments and the increasing use of temporary (interim) executives.

This, along with the greater use of non-executive directors and advisers by a variety of companies, suggests that the 1990s will produce new employment opportunities for mature managers.

Your own business

During your working life you may have harboured the dream of running your own business when you retire. This is not something to be undertaken lightly and you must ask yourself some serious questions.

Have you got what it takes to run your own business? Do you have a good idea, something unique which you know you can sell?

You will also need the technical knowledge and experience

to run the business and be satisfied it will be profitable – remembering that you will have to draw a reasonable remuneration.

And do you have the finance available in a form which will not place you and your spouse at risk in your old age?

The next step should be to prepare a business plan ready for discussion with your accountant, bank manager and others you expect to finance or take part in the business.

One obvious business activity for professional or technically qualified people is to set up a consultancy to provide advice and services in the field where their expertise lies.

This can take the form of an operation in which you have one or two clients (such as your former business) or a freelance consultancy which will provide services to a wider range of clients.

Your accountant will advise you about the expenses you can charge against income for tax purposes. For example, if you work from home a proportion of the running costs of your house may be deductible. You will also need to be aware of the requirements to register for VAT when your turnover exceeds the threshold (currently £35,000 per annum).

It is increasingly recognised that those approaching retirement need advice. Many financial institutions and commercial companies, such as Prudential, Ford, BP, THF and Laing, provide expert counselling.

There are also specialist organisations which run courses and seminars for others. In particular, the Pre-Retirement Association of 19 Undine Street, London SW17, which issues a directory of pre-retirement courses in the UK.

These courses cover a wide range of subjects, including re-training, demographic trends, financial planning, housing and the use of leisure.

One's approach to retirement clearly requires careful consideration. What must be resisted is any temptation to enter into commitments which may jeopardise one's hard-earned comfort and security.

SMALL FIRMS ORGANISATIONS

THE ASSOCIATION OF BRITISH
CHAMBERS OF COMMERCE
212a Shaftesbury Avenue
London WC2H 8EW
Tel 071-240 5831
Fax 071-379 6331
President: Sir James Ackers
Director General: R.G. Taylor
Secretary: Miss Jocelyn Jackson-
Matthews

ASSOCIATION OF INDEPENDENT
BUSINESS
133 Copeland Road
London SE15 3SP
Tel 071-277 5158
Fax 071-358 1049
Chairman: David Selby
Secretary: J.B.M. Donnelan

THE FORUM OF PRIVATE
BUSINESS
Ruskin Chambers
Drury Lane
Knutsford
Cheshire WA16 6HA
Tel (0565) 4467
Fax (0565) 50059
Chairman: Les Hales
Chief Executive: Stan Mendham

THE INSTITUTE OF DIRECTORS
116 Pall Mall
London SW1Y 5ED
Tel 071-839 1233
Fax 071-930 1949
Head of Policy Unit: Dr Ann Robinson
Administrator, Small Firms: Brian
Moxey

THE NATIONAL CHAMBER OF
TRADE
Enterprise House
59 Castle Street
Reading
Berkshire RG1 7SN
Tel (0734) 566744
Fax (0734) 567963
President: R. Lang
Director General: Bernard Tennant

CBI SMALLER FIRMS COUNCIL
Centre Point
103 New Oxford Street
London WC1A 1DU
Tel 071-379 7400
Fax 071-240 1578
Director of Regions and SFC: Miss Sonia
Elkin
Deputy Director: Andy Scott

THE UNION OF INDEPENDENT
COMPANIES
Bradfield Road
London E16 2AY
Tel 071-476 3171
Fax 071-474 0098
Chairman: James Scarlett
General Secretary: Richard Maurice

UNITED KINGDOM SCIENCE PARK
ASSOCIATION
Barclays Venture Centre
Sir Williams Lyon Road
Coventry
CV4 7EX
Tel (0203) 418535
Fax (0203) 410156
Administrator: John Hands

THE NATIONAL FEDERATION OF
SELF-EMPLOYED AND SMALL
BUSINESSES LIMITED
140 Lower Marsh
Westminster Bridge
London SE1 7AE
Tel 071-928 9272
Fax 071-401 2544
Chairman: Bill Knox
Secretary: George Needham